DISLOYALTY IN THE
CONFEDERACY

DISLOYALTY IN THE CONFEDERACY

By

GEORGIA LEE TATUM, Ph.D.

CHAPEL HILL
THE UNIVERSITY OF NORTH CAROLINA PRESS
1934

COPYRIGHT, 1934, BY
THE UNIVERSITY OF NORTH CAROLINA PRESS

PRINTED IN THE UNITED STATES OF AMERICA BY
THE SEEMAN PRESS, DURHAM, NORTH CAROLINA
THIS BOOK WAS DIGITALLY PRINTED.

To

THE MEMORY OF

MY MOTHER AND FATHER

WHO INSPIRED IN ME
A LOVE FOR HISTORY

PREFACE

THIS STUDY, prepared as a doctoral dissertation at Vanderbilt University, Nashville, Tennessee, is an attempt to portray the widespread disaffection in the Confederate States and the attempts, during the War between the States, to bring about peace. Until recently, many historians, as well as people in general, have commonly accepted the idea that every man, woman, and child in the South stood loyally behind Jefferson Davis and the Stars and Bars in support of the Confederacy. Despite the fact that out of a population of about eight million whites, six hundred thousand offered their services to the Confederacy in 1861, and also the fact that the staunch, unswerving loyalty of Southerners during the war will continue to rouse admiration, there was, in 1861, a small number, which by 1865 had increased to a potent minority, that did nothing to aid the Confederacy and much to injure it. While many showed their disaffection only by refusing to fight, many others organized not only for self-protection but also for the destruction of the Confederacy. Before the end of the war, there was much disaffection in every state, and many of the disloyal had formed into bands —in some states into well organized, active societies, with signs, oaths, grips, and passwords. In the present study, an attempt has been made to discover the causes for this movement, the classes that participated in it, and the purpose and work of the organizations.

The writer realizes the difficulties involved in the use of the words "disloyal" and "disloyalty." She is fully aware of the fact that what one section of the country execrated as disloyalty, another section of the country praised as loyalty. She found in her sources, both primary and secondary, innumerable instances of warring points of view; of diametrically opposite terms applied to the same phenomenon; of violently contrasting motives imputed to the same act. In the interests of directness and clarity, the following usage was decided upon: the term "disloyal" is applied to persons living in the Confederacy, who not only refused to support the Confederate government but who also appeared to be actively working against it. The term "disaffection" is used more broadly to characterize those who, though opposed to the Confederacy, were, on the whole, passive. The term "unionist" is applied, as it was in certain sources, to those who, like many of the East Tennesseans, were from the first strong advocates of the Union. If at times such unionists have been characterized as disloyal, it has been done because they were overwhelmingly regarded as disloyal by the members of their community, and were so unequivocally characterized as disloyal in the sources consulted that any attempt to determine allegiance seemed likely to cause further confusion.

No reflection is meant to be cast upon anyone who either passively or actively supported the Union; but it is hoped that the study will help to dispel the false idea that the inhabitants of the seceded states were a unit in supporting the "Lost Cause."

Louisiana has not been included in this study because it fell into the hands of the Federals in the second year of the war and was practically lost to the Confederacy. It is a question whether Tennessee, especially East Tennessee, should have been included. But despite the facts that a majority of East Tennesseans never favored secession, that many of their leaders openly declared for the Union and consistently supported it throughout the war, and that the Confederate government in the state collapsed in 1862, it has been included, because the state did secede and because the strategic location of so large a group of Union sympathizers certainly weakened the Confederacy. Furthermore, some of the unionists in that section professed loyalty to the Confederacy but worked secretly for its downfall—an example of the difficulties involved in characterizing such people accurately.

In view of the almost insoluble complexities of the subject, and its powerful emotional connotations, the author has been content to present the facts as she found them and to leave conclusions to the reader.

The principal materials used in the study were the official records of the Union and Confederate armies; diaries, memoirs, and reminiscences of participants in the War between the States; biographies and general and special accounts of the period. An examination of Mississippi newspaper files disclosed the fact that the type of material sought could not be found in newspapers.

I desire to express my appreciation to the following libraries for the use of their various collections: Library of the State of Tennessee, The Tennessee Historical Society Library, The George Peabody College Library, and the Carnegie Library, Nashville, Tennessee; The Mississippi State Library and the Department of Archives and History, Jackson, Mississippi; the D. A. R. Library, Cleveland, Mississippi; and especially to Vanderbilt University Library and its staff for much help and many courtesies extended to me during my work there.

I wish to acknowledge my indebtedness and to express my deep sense of gratitude to Professor Frank L. Owsley, of Vanderbilt University, who first interested me in this subject and who has given generously of his time in directing, criticizing, and encouraging me in research and writing; to the late Professor Walter L. Fleming, of Vanderbilt University, who, in the absence of Professor Owsley, directed this study for one year and was always ready to offer criticism and encouragement; to Professor W. C. Binkley, of Vanderbilt University, who read the manuscript and proposed valuable suggestions as to organization and arrangement of material; to Professor E. M. Violette, of Louisiana State University; to Professor Evelyn Hammett, of Mississippi Delta State Teachers College, and to other friends who read the manuscript and offered helpful criticisms.

GEORGIA LEE TATUM

Mississippi Delta State Teachers College
Cleveland, Mississippi
March, 1934

TABLE OF CONTENTS

CHAPTER	PAGE
Preface	vii
I. The Causes of Disloyalty	3
II. The Development of Peace Societies	24
III. Disaffection West of the Mississippi	36
IV. The Peace Society in Alabama	54
V. Disaffection in Georgia, Florida, and Mississippi	73
VI. The Heroes of America and Disaffection in the Carolinas	107
VII. Unionism in East Tennessee and Southwest Virginia	143
Selected Bibliography	167
Index	171

DISLOYALTY IN THE CONFEDERACY

CHAPTER I
THE CAUSES OF DISLOYALTY

THE SOUTH presented so solid a front at the beginning of the Civil War that, out of a population of eight million whites, six hundred thousand men offered their services to the Confederacy during the first year of the war.[1] Despite this fact, however, there were a few at the beginning of the war and many before the end that did not stand loyally behind Jefferson Davis and the Stars and Bars in support of the Confederacy. While many showed their disaffection only by refusing to fight for, or to give active support to, the Confederacy, others went so far as to organize not only for self-protection but also for injury to the Confederacy and aid to the Union. Before the close of the war there was considerable disaffection in every state of the Confederacy, and many of the disloyal formed into bands—in some states into well organized secret treasonable societies, of which the most potent and pernicious were the Order of the Heroes of America, the Peace Society, and the Peace and Constitutional Society.

There were various reasons for this widespread disaffection in the Confederacy. Although it undoubtedly had its inception among those who, for one reason or another, opposed secession or were apathetic in 1861, it was increased as a result of certain laws passed by the Confederate Congress; by the conflict between the state and Confederate authorities over the enforcement of these laws; by the hardships of war; by war weariness and the seeming hopelessness of the Confederate cause after 1863; and by the state

[1] Frank Lawrence Owsley, "Defeatism in the Confederacy," *North Carolina Historical Review*, III (July, 1926), 446.

rights peace movement led by Alexander H. Stephens, Joseph E. Brown, Zebulon Vance, and other state rights champions.

Opposition to Secession

A brief survey of the secession movement at the beginning of the war reveals the fact that there was considerable opposition to secession in most of the southern states in 1861, and that the sections which opposed withdrawal from the Union at that time were the sections in which there was most disaffection shown during the war and in which the most powerful and dangerous disloyal bands and treasonable peace societies flourished.

In general, those that opposed leaving the Union in 1861 were old-line Whigs, who were either outspoken unionists or unionists at heart, the up-country element, the foreign element, and many others who hoped for an ultimate peaceful settlement of the questions causing trouble. Much of the opposition to secession was due to an intense sectionalism, which had arisen out of the different social and economic structures resulting from geographical environment. Although many of the up-country dwellers hoped some day to own slaves, they had relatively few at that time, and therefore they had little to lose by emancipation. This sectionalism had manifested itself, all the way from Maryland to Texas, in an unjust distribution of representation and had engendered a bitter feeling against the small group of slave owners who kept the political power in their own hands and often abused it.[2]

The only state in which there was not, in 1861, considerable opposition to withdrawal from the Union was South Carolina, the first state to withdraw. In Virginia, Tennessee, Alabama, Arkansas, and Georgia, opposition came mainly

[2] *Ibid.*, pp. 446-47; Charles H. McCarthy, *Lincoln's Plan of Reconstruction*, p. 97; J. M. Callahan, *Semi-Centennial History of West Virginia*, pp. 135-36, 138-40.

from the up-country element, the unionists, and those who hoped for an ultimate peaceful settlement.

In Virginia practically all of the people in the western part of the state were either ardent unionists or were apathetic. In fact, the unionists were so numerous that they succeeded in separating the northwestern part of the state from Virginia and in forming West Virginia, which gave no support to the Confederacy.[3] Although the southwestern section of the state, in which not more than one-fourth of the people favored secession,[4] did not separate from Virginia, it evinced enough disaffection to furnish a birthplace for treasonable organizations, a refuge for renegades from other Confederate states, and a source of opposition to the attempted enforcement of laws by the Confederate government. Many of the mountaineers had no interest in the questions of the day and asked only to be let alone. Geographic and economic conditions made the people west of the mountains more in sympathy with the North than with the South.[5]

The eastern part of Tennessee, which after 1861 gave practically no support to the Confederacy and which served as a refuge for the disloyal from all over the South, was almost solid for the Union. There was a strong Union element elsewhere in the state. During the campaign of 1861 "Parson" Brownlow and other prominent Union leaders in the mountain districts said that if the southern people attempted to carry out "their nefarious designs to destroy the Republic," they would have to walk over "the dead

[3] *American Annual Cyclopedia* (1861), pp. 738, 739, 742-43. (Hereafter cited as *A. C.*); James Ford Rhodes, *History of the United States*, III, 322-23; Oliver P. Temple, *East Tennessee and the Civil War*, p. 163; Robert White "West Virginia," in Clement A. Evans, *Confederate Military History*, II, 10-12.

[4] *A. C.* (1861), p. 739; Callahan, *op. cit.*, p. 152. In what is now West Virginia the vote was ten to one against the Virginia ordinance of secession.

[5] *Ibid.*, pp. 139-40; McCarthy, *op. cit.*, p. 97; White, in Evans, *op. cit.*, p. 6; Rhodes, *op. cit.*, pp. 322-23; *A. C.* (1861), p. 743.

bodies of East Tennesseans slain in battle."[6] When the people voted on the question of holding a convention, and electing delegates thereto should one be held, the returns of the election showed a majority of 11,875 against a convention;[7] and a total of 91,803 votes for Union delegates and 24,749 for secession delegates. Every section of the state returned a large majority for Union delegates, though West Tennessee returned a majority for the convention.[8]

Despite the seemingly strong opposition to secession in Tennessee, when President Lincoln called for troops the governor refused to send them and urged that the state secede.[9] Instead of holding a convention, the legislature provided for the submitting of a "Declaration of Independence" to the vote of the people.[10] The returns showed a majority for the declaration. The unionists charged fraud in the election, and East Tennessee attempted to separate from the rest of the state.[11]

Perhaps much of the opposition in East Tennessee was due to a few Union leaders who not only began early to stir up sentiment for the Union and continued to do so throughout the war,[12] but who also, in order to arouse hostility toward the Confederacy, created a bitter feeling between the rural and the town people.[13]

In North Alabama, where the Peace Society flourished and where, before the close of the war, in half the counties in the state deserters and stragglers could go and come without fear of arrest,[14] the majority of the people opposed

---

[6] Thomas W. Humes, *The Loyal Mountaineers of Tennessee*, pp. 80-81; William G. Brownlow, *Sketches of the Rise, Progress, and Decline of Secession (Parson Brownlow's Book)*, p. 67. (Hereafter cited as *Parson Brownlow's Book*); A. C. (1861), p. 677; Temple, *op. cit.*, pp. 162, 200.

[7] A. C. (1861), pp. 677, 678.   [9] *Ibid.*, p. 678.
[8] *Ibid.*, pp. 677, 678.   [10] *Ibid.*, p. 680.
[11] *Ibid.*, p. 681; Edward McPherson, *Political History of the United States of America During the Great Rebellion*, p. 5; *Parson Brownlow's Book*, p. 139.
[12] Temple, *op. cit.*, pp. 200-1, 340-65.   [13] Humes, *op. cit.*, pp. 105, 118, 340-45.
[14] *The War of the Rebellion: A Compilation of the Official Records of the Union*

leaving the Union in 1861. Every county in North Alabama sent to the convention coöperationists, that is, people who either wished to coöperate within the Union and force their rights from the Federal government, or were in favor of making plans to coöperate with the other southern states before they withdrew from the Union.[15] William R. Smith, Robert J. Jemison, David P. Lewis, Jeremiah Clemens, and Nicholas Davis were the leaders of the North Alabama coöperationists.[16] Most of the so-called coöperationists were Whigs, and Smith, Jemison, and Davis had been prominent unionists in 1851.[17] Although there was not a single strong appeal made for the Union in the convention of 1861,[18] the coöperationists did all they could to obstruct the work of the immediate secessionists.[19] Most of the North Alabama delegates denied the sovereignty of the convention[20] and said that they believed their constituents would refuse to abide by an order of secession unless it were submitted to them for ratification or rejection. When William Yancey denounced the people of North Alabama as traitors, tories, and rebels and declared that they ought to be coerced into a submission to the decree of the convention, Nicholas Davis, of Madison, angrily replied that the secessionists might attempt coercion but North Alabama would meet them at the foot of the mountains and decide the issue at the point of the bayonet.[21]

Thirty-one of the votes cast against the ordinance of secession were cast by delegates from that section.[22] Thirty-three of the delegates from North Alabama, two of whom had voted for the ordinance, refused to sign it, though

and the Confederate Armies (Washington, 1880-1901), ser. IV, vol. III, p. 1065. (Hereafter cited as *O. R.*); Walter Lynwood Fleming, *Civil War and Reconstruction in Alabama*, p. 53.

[15] *Ibid.*, p. 28.
[16] *Ibid.*, pp. 21, 29.
[17] *Ibid.*, pp. 15-16, 403n.
[18] *Ibid.*, p. 34.
[19] *Ibid.*, pp. 31, 35, 37, 40, 53.
[20] *Ibid.*, p. 35.
[21] *Ibid.*, p. 54; *A. C.* (1861), p. 10.
[22] Fleming, *op. cit.*, p. 109.

they said that they would abide by it. However, they published far and wide an address to the people in which they attempted to justify their opposition and refusal to sign, and this gave the impression that they considered the action of the convention illegal.[23]

There was a small element of the population in the mountains and sandhills of that section which was not in any way concerned with the questions before the people, but which always opposed any measure supported by the southern part of the state. Its representative, C. C. Sheets, of Winston, was one of the delegates who refused to sign the ordinance[24] and who during the war went over to the enemy.[25] Professor Fleming says concerning the opposition of North Alabama: "There were many indications that the opposition was more sectional and personal than political. It is safe to state for North Alabama that had the Black Belt declared for the Union, that section would have voted for secession."[26]

Nicholas Davis and Jeremiah Clemens also went over to the enemy during the war.[27]

Northwest Arkansas, in which there was much disloyalty during the war, was almost solidly against secession.[28] In fact, the Union sentiment was so strong in the state that no secession movement took place within its borders until December 20, 1860, at which time a commissioner from Alabama addressed the legislature on the subject. The

---

[23] *Ibid.*, p. 55; *A. C.* (1861), p. 11; *O. R.*, ser. IV, vol. I, pp. 68-70. Later, nine of the thirty-three signed the ordinance.—Fleming, *op. cit.*, p. 55.

[24] *Ibid.*, pp. 54, 110.

[25] *Ibid.*, p. 126.   [26] *Ibid.*, p. 31n.

[27] *Ibid.*, pp. 35, 109, 125, 126, 403; A. B. Moore, *History of Alabama and Her People*, p. 545.

[28] A. W. Bishop, *Loyalty on the Frontier, or Sketches of Union Men of the Southwest*, p. 21. Bishop, an ardent unionist, soon after the war began joined the Federals at Springfield, Missouri, and was made lieutenant colonel of the First Arkansas Cavalry Volunteers, most of whom were Arkansas unionists who asked to be sent back to Arkansas to fight for their homes and the Union.

election of Lincoln was not considered a sufficient cause for leaving the Union and men of every party favored all honorable efforts to preserve the Union. Demonstrations to the contrary were considered the work of an extreme minority.[29]

When on February 18, 1861, an election to select delegates to a convention was held, the returns showed a Union majority of 5,699, the total vote being 41,553. In the convention in the early part of March a conditional ordinance of secession was defeated, and at Van Buren and Fort Smith, which later proved to be centers of unionism, a salute of thirty-nine guns was fired in honor of the thirty-nine men who voted against the ordinance.[30] Despite the strong opposition to secession, when Lincoln called on the governor for troops and he refused to send them, the convention reassembled on May 6 and decided, with only one dissenting vote, to leave the Union.[31] But the ardent Union element in the northwestern section of the state,[32] especially the frontiersmen and mountaineers, many of whom were Irish, immediately began to organize for resistance to the Confederacy; and as will be seen later, the first treasonable peace society in the Confederacy was organized in this section.

Although most of the people in Georgia believed in the right of secession, many of them did not wish to leave the Union in 1861. The secession convention included nearly every well known public man in the state and represented nearly every shade of public opinion.[33] Alexander

[29] *A. C.* (1861), p. 22; David Y. Thomas, *Arkansas in War and Reconstruction, 1861-1874*, p. 44.
[30] *A. C.* (1861), p. 22; Bishop, *op. cit.*, p. 21.
[31] *A. C.* (1861), p. 23; Bishop, *op. cit.*, pp. 22, 25, 26; Thomas, *op. cit.*, pp. 70, 82.
Isaac Murphy refused to remain at home and, partly because of love for the Union, joined the Union Army.—Bishop, pp. 26-27.
[32] In general the mountain counties were white.—Thomas, *op. cit.*, p. 13.
[33] Lucian Knight, *Georgia's Landmarks, Memorials, and Legends*, II, 562; *A. C.* (1861), p. 336.

H. Stephens and H. V. Johnson, leaders of the coöperationists and unionists in the convention, insisted that there was no cause for secession at that time and argued that Georgia could secure better terms in the Union than out of it.[34] More than one-third of the delegates voted against secession,[35] but, in order to present a united front to the world, they all signed the ordinance of secession.[36]

Many people remained unreconciled to the withdrawal from the Union. In practically every mountain county where there had been bitter opposition to secession, many not only refused to lower the Stars and Stripes after the ordinance was passed, but in Jasper, Pickens County, a United States flag was deliberately raised on a pole and floated for several weeks in defiance of the Confederate authority.[37]

Throughout North Carolina there were many zealous unionists, and until Lincoln called for troops the large majority of the people opposed secession. When the question of a convention to consider secession was submitted to the popular vote, it was defeated by a majority of 651 votes,[38] although W. W. Holden, Jonathan Worth, Dr. J. T. Leach, Josiah Turner, and other Union leaders, hoping to place the state definitely on the side of the Union, had urged the people to vote for a convention.[39] Delegates to a convention, should one be held, were voted on at the same time. One hundred twenty delegates were elected, only sixty-eight of whom were secessionists.[40] But when Lincoln called for North Carolina's quota of troops and the governor replied, "You can get no troops from North

[34] *Ibid.*, pp. 563-64.
[35] *Tribune Almanac* (1861), p. 41; *A. C.* (1861), p. 338.
[36] *Knight*, p. 565; *A. C.* (1861), p. 339.
[37] Avery, *The History of the State of Georgia from 1850 to 1881*, p. 187; *A. C.* (1861), p. 339. This incident is described in greater detail on pp. 73-74 below.
[38] J. G. DeRoulhac Hamilton, *Reconstruction in North Carolina*, p. 20.
[39] W. W. Holden, *Memoirs*, II, 15.
[40] Hamilton, *op. cit.*, p. 20; *A. C.* (1861), p. 538.

Carolina,"[41] "not a person in the state advocated anything but separation" and in the convention "every delegate present" voted to withdraw from the Union.[42] W. W. Holden, who during the war became a member of the Order of the Heroes of America, said that the secessionists threw their hats in the air and rejoiced when the ordinance of secession was passed, but that the conservatives—as the unionists styled themselves in the convention—remained very quiet and looked depressed.[43] Not only Holden but also other Union leaders in the convention became active in stirring up opposition to Davis and encouraging disloyalty during the war; and the Heroes of America had a decided influence in the state.

In Texas, where many disloyal bands were formed during the war, there was an element made up largely of old-time Whigs and Germans who bitterly opposed secession and never became reconciled to the Confederacy.[44] When Governor Samuel Houston, an ardent unionist, refused to call an extra session of the legislature to provide for a convention to consider secession, sixty-one secessionists issued a call to the people to hold an election for the purpose of selecting delegates to a convention.[45] Because of strong Union sentiment, nearly one-half of the counties held no election. In many of the counties in which elections were held, unionists refused to vote. Travis County, in which Austin is located and in which many Germans lived, had 1,011 votes, but only 342 votes were cast.[46] Practically all of the Germans who voted and the people in the regions

[41] *O. R.*, ser. I, vol. I, p. 486; *A. C.* (1861), pp. 538-39.
[42] Hamilton, *op. cit.*, pp. 25, 30.
[43] W. W. Holden, *Memoirs*, II, 17.   [44] *A. C.* (1861), pp. 686-87.
[45] *Ibid.*, p. 687; C. W. Ramsdell, *Reconstruction in Texas*, pp. 14, 15; George P. Garrison, *Texas; A Contest of Civilizations*, p. 285; *The Mississippian*, of February 1, 1860, said: "Governor Houston 'is an eager aspirant for Federal honors' and therefore is ready to 'sacrifice the rights and interests of his own section to win favor of the anti-slavery majority.'"
[46] *A. C.* (1861), p. 688.

westward from Austin and south of the Red River, who had not been bothered by Indian raids for several years, voted almost solidly against secession. On the other hand, the failure of the United States government to protect the northern and western counties from the Indians and the report that the Abolitionists in Kansas were encouraging Indian raids and the burning of the towns on the border, alarmed the people of that section so that they, hoping the new Confederacy might protect them, voted almost solidly for secession.[47] Under these circumstances it is obvious that the secessionists controlled the convention.[48]

On February 5, by a vote of 166 to 7, the convention passed an ordinance of secession. When it was submitted to the people on February 23, the votes cast for the ordinance were about three to one.[49] The vote at the presidential election in November, 1860, was as follows: Lincoln, none; Douglas, none; Breckenridge, 47,548; Bell, 15,438.[50] It is interesting to note that the Breckenridge vote was considerably heavier than the vote for secession in 1861, while the Bell vote, which one may safely conclude represented fairly well the unionist vote, corresponded more closely to the vote against secession. The unionists declared the elections were unfair and insisted that the majority of the people were against secession,[51] an estimate which is hardly probable, although, as later developments show, the opponents of secession were many.

In Mississippi there was a respectable minority of co-operationists and unionists, most of whom were old-time Whigs who opposed secession. Of the ninety-nine delegates elected to the secession convention, about one-fourth were co-operationists and unionists. Most of the unionists had

---

[47] Ramsdell, "The Frontier and Secession," *Studies in Southern History and Politics*, pp. 75-77.
[48] *A. C.* (1861), p. 688.
[49] *Tribune Almanac* (1862), p. 42; Ramsdell, *Reconstruction in Texas*, pp. 16, 19.
[50] *A. C.* (1861), p. 689. [51] Ramsdell, *Reconstruction in Texas*, p. 19.

positive instructions to vote against secession. However, there were only fifteen votes cast against the ordinance. Among the prominent leaders of the opposition to secession were Judges William L. Sharkey, George Poindexter, J. S. Yerger, and ex-Governor A. G. Brown, all of whom were old-time Whigs.[52]

After the fall of Vicksburg, these and other unionists took the oath of allegiance to the United States and began to lead a peace movement on the basis of a return to the Union,[53] a movement which found many adherents not only among those who had been lukewarm or disloyal from the beginning, but among those who had been loyal up to that time.

Opposition to Confederate Laws

Disloyalty was increased when the Confederate Congress found it necessary to pass, during the course of the war, conscription laws, impressment and tax-in-kind acts, and a law giving Jefferson Davis the right to suspend the writ of habeas corpus in order to deal with disloyalty. For various reasons these laws were resented and opposed by many people; and when the state authorities denounced them as being unjust, tyrannical, and unconstitutional, and many times either evaded them or defiantly refused to obey them, disaffection among the people was naturally strengthened.

Conscription Acts

The first conscription act, passed April 16, 1862, provided for the enrollment of all white males in the Confederate States between the ages of eighteen and thirty-five

---

[52] James W. Garner, *Reconstruction in Mississippi*, p. 5; *A. C.* (1861), pp. 473-74; Thomas H. Woods, "A Sketch of the Mississippi Secession Convention of 1861," *Publications of the Mississippi Historical Society*, VI (1902), 93, 98.

[53] Woods, *op. cit.*, pp. 98, 101; *The Mississippian*, May 2, 1860; *ibid.*, August 8, 1860; Garner, *Reconstruction in Mississippi*, pp. 51, 53, 56.

and placed them at the disposal of the president during the war.[54] This law was very unpopular throughout the South. The people who were willing to enter the army if necessary, considered it very odious to be forced to fight for their liberty,[55] while those who, for various reasons, did not wish to enter the army, naturally opposed being forced to enter it. The poor man found a further grievance in the clause that allowed a conscript to furnish a substitute, since this enabled a rich man to remain at home if he so desired.[56] Many soldiers in the army argued that if an exempt were fit for service he should come to the army without being hired.[57] The substitute clause furnished the basis for the accusation that the war was a "rich man's war and a poor man's fight."[58] Though the substitute clause was repealed before the close of the war,[59] the dissatisfaction and the charge continued. Unionists and other disaffected people wishing to alienate the poorer classes, put out many untrue reports of avoidance of military duty by the ruling class.[60] The exemption laws gave further grounds for complaint.[61] When the exemption law providing for the exemption of one person as owner or overseer of each twenty Negroes—and later of each fifteen Negroes—was passed,[62]

[54] *O. R.*, ser. IV, vol. I, p. 1095.

[55] H. V. Johnson, "Documents from the Autobiography of Herschel V. Johnson, 1856-1867," *American Historical Review*, XXX (January, 1925), 332.

[56] *O. R.*, ser. IV, vol. I, p. 1096; J. B. Jones, *A Rebel War Clerk's Diary at the Confederate States Capital*, I, 30, 218-19. (Hereafter cited as Jones, *Diary*); N. W. Stephenson, *The Day of the Confederacy*, p. 103; J. C. Schwab, *The Confederate States of America, 1861-1865*, p. 196; A. C. (1862), p. 246.

[57] Schwab, *op. cit.*, p. 196; T. C. DeLeon, *Four Years in Rebel Capitals*, p. 178.

[58] Professor Fleming says the complaint of "a rich man's war and a poor man's fight" as well as the criticism of the "twenty-negro law" originated with the disloyal class of north Alabama.—*Op. cit.*, pp. 101-2.

[59] *O. R.*, ser. IV, vol. III, pp. 12, 24.

[60] Stephenson, *The Day of the Confederacy*, p. 103.

[61] *O. R.*, ser. IV, vol. I, pp. 976-77, 1084, 1104, 1110, 1123-24, 1121, 1174; vol. II, pp. 126-28, 160-62; vol. III, *passim*; ser. IV, vol. I, pp. 1021-22.

[62] *Ibid.*, ser. IV, vol. II, pp. 162, 553, 690-91.

the men of small property joined in the cry of "a rich man's war and a poor man's fight."[63]

CRITICISM OF CONSCRIPTION ACTS BY STATE AUTHORITIES

This feeling of injustice and disaffection was further increased by the criticism and opposition offered by the state authorities who wished to retain control of their armies in order not only to provide for local defense and to commission the officers of their troops, but also to retain all men whom they deemed necessary to do work for the state.[64]

Governor Joseph E. Brown, of Georgia, the only governor who from the beginning openly defied the Confederate government and refused any coöperation whatsoever in the execution of the acts,[65] wrote Davis that he considered them unfair, oppressive, and unconstitutional; that he would have nothing to do with the enrollment of conscripts in Georgia; that he forbade the removal from the state of any officer whom he considered necessary to maintain the state government; and that he could not consent to commit Georgia to a policy which was in his judgment subversive of her sovereignty and at war with all the principles for the support of which she had entered the war.[66]

When the conscription law was later extended to include the men between thirty-five and forty-five years of age, Governor Brown said, "No act of the government of the United States . . . struck a blow at constitutional liberty so fell as has been stricken by the conscription acts."[67] After demanding that no more conscripts be enrolled in Georgia, he informed Davis that the Georgians "having entered into

[63] *Ibid.*, pp. 286-87; ser. I, vol. XVII, pt. II, p. 790; Jones, *Diary*, II, 30; Moore, *Conscription and Conflict in the Confederacy*, pp. 71, 143, 144; Stephenson, *op. cit.*, p. 103.

[64] *O. R.*, ser. IV, vol. III, pp. 463-64, 307, 425-28, 817-18, 820, 821-22, 823, 824, 976-79, 848-49, 530, 197-98; ser. IV, vol. I, p. 1123; Moore, *op. cit.*, pp. 94-95.

[65] DeLeon, *op. cit.*, p. 179.

[66] *O. R.*, ser. IV, vol. I, pp. 1116-20; *A. C.* (1862), p. 244.

[67] *O. R.*, ser. IV, vol. II, p. 131; Stephenson, *op. cit.*, p. 66.

the revolution free men," intended "to emerge from it free men."[68]

Though the other governors, with the exception of Vance of North Carolina, had not offered such bitter opposition to the conscription laws, they had objected to them and protested against the enrollment of certain classes of people. Despite these laws, all of the governors had enrolled many conscripts in their local defense organizations, which they had proceeded to build up as soon as their state armies had been swept away by the first conscription act.[69]

Brown claimed the right to withdraw Georgia troops from the Confederate armies. After the battle of Chicamauga he demanded that certain Georgia troops, which he claimed he had furnished the Confederacy for only six months, be allowed to return home to attend to their crops and look after other business. When his demand was refused, he became very indignant, accused the government of breaking faith with the soldiers, and expressed a doubt as to whether he could raise any more troops for the Confederacy. In 1864, when Sherman was before Atlanta, he did call home and furlough the Georgia militia that had been under Joseph E. Johnston.[70]

While these are only a few instances of the innumerable controversies which occurred between Davis and Brown over conscription, they are sufficient to illustrate the conflict between the state and Confederate authorities which occurred in Georgia and elsewhere on this question.[71] By

---

[68] O. R., ser. IV, vol. II, p. 131.

[69] Owsley, "Local Defense and the Overthrow of the Confederacy," *Mississippi Valley Historical Review*, XI (March, 1925), 500-2.

[70] For the controversy between Jefferson Davis and Jos. E. Brown over conscription see: O. R., ser. IV, vol. I, pp. 1082-85, 1100, 1116-20, 1126, 1128-30, 1133-38, 1154, 1156-68; vol. II, pp. 2, 3, 10-13, 128-31, 216, 217, 952-53, 823-24; vol. III, pp. 61-62; Owsley, *State Rights in the Confederacy*, p. 48.

[71] For similar controversies in other states see: O. R., ser. IV, vol. II, pp. 464, 307, 425-26, 398-99, 746, 596; vol. III, pp. 307, 425-28, 530, 746, 466, 256, 463, 322-23, 817, 819, 821, 848-49.

1864 the necessity for producers at home and the increased sensitiveness on the part of the states as to their rights to maintain state troops caused much dissatisfaction and opposition in every state, and as many conscripts as possible were retained by the states.[72]

In North Carolina, where the opposition to the conscription acts was almost as bitter as in Georgia, the courts freely granted writs of habeas corpus to both conscripts and deserters. Governor Vance refused to bring any pressure to bear upon the courts, though he knew the practice was causing many to desert from the army.[73] In fact, he, as well as other governors, encouraged desertion and evasion of the conscription laws by requesting Davis to allow the enrollment in local defense organizations of conscripts who were unwilling to enter the Confederate army. The argument of the goverors was that the Confederacy would never be able to get that class of men anyway.[74]

Naturally such bitter opposition to Davis and the conscription laws on the part of the governors and other leading men of the Confederacy not only increased the disaffection in the South but also encouraged many to use every available means of keeping out of the army and—if these failed—of getting out of it at the first opportunity.

Criticism of Impressment Laws

A grievance of the farmers, which was used to increase disaffection, was the impressment laws. Under these laws slaves, wagons, livestock, and provisions needed for the army[75] were impressed, and the farmers were compelled

---

[72] Owsley, "Local Defense and the Overthrow of the Confederacy," *Mississippi Valley Historical Review*, XI (March, 1925), 514-19; *O. R.*, ser. IV, vol. II, pp. 775-76; vol. III, pp. 172-74, 821-22, 903-4, 307, 309, 1162-64, 740, 823-24; ser. I, vol. LII, pt. II, p. 726.

[73] *O. R.*, ser. I, vol. LI, pt. II, p. 714.

[74] *Ibid.*, ser. IV, vol. II, pp. 603-4.

[75] *Ibid.*, vol. II, pp. 30, 211-12, 469-71; *Confederate Statutes at Large*, p. 8.

to accept the price fixed by the impressment committee commissioners, which was always below the market price.[76] Immediately after the first impressment law was passed, protests from farmers[77] and state authorities were sent to Richmond.[78] A few of the typical complaints will suffice to show the reasons for the general dissatisfaction with these laws and their consequent effect upon the attitude of the people toward the Confederacy.

The governor of Florida said agents were violating the law by demanding all the produce.[79] He considered it his duty to interpose "to protect the rights, lives, and liberty of the citizens" against the military order of the Confederate officers who were enforcing the law.[80] Governor Brown complained not only that the impressment agents were taking all of the supplies from some communities leaving little for the people to live on, and passing over entirely other persons and neighborhoods, but also that many unauthorized persons had resorted to impressment as a convenient method of stealing and robbing. He urged the people to resist unless the officer could show a proper certificate. In Brown's opinion the impressment act was causing much dissatisfaction among the people and was leading to disloyalty.[81]

The South Carolina legislature passed resolutions which embodied the same charges that Governor Brown had made and added that the supplies set aside for tax-in-kind were sometimes not called for, while the impressment agents took other supplies more conveniently located.[82] Other legis-

[76] *A. C.* (1863), pp. 207, 447; *O. R.*, ser. IV, vol. II, pp. 944, 559-61.

[77] *A. C.* (1863), p. 206.

[78] *O. R.*, ser. IV, vol. II, p. 975, vol. III, pp. 43-45, 37, 560-61, 446, 690; Jones, *Diary*, I, 201.

[79] *O. R.*, ser. IV, vol. II, pp. 973-74.

[80] *Ibid.*, p. 975.

[81] *O. R.*, ser. IV, vol. II, pp. 943-44, 404-5, 988, 989, 1023; *A. C.* (1861), p. 447; *Natchez Daily Courier*, April 14, 1863, quoting from the *Augusta Chronicle*.

[82] *O. R.*, ser. IV, vol. II, pp. 863-64, 875-77.

latures passed resolutions similar in character to those of South Carolina.[83]

Robert Toombs further increased the disaffection by declaring, in an address to the Georgia legislature, that the law was in violation of the fundamental principle of the Constitution, which required all burdens to be uniform and just. The impressment act, he said, was neither uniform nor just because the "capitalists, merchants, manufacturers, speculators, and extortioners," who had remained at home and made money during the war, paid none of the tax. Their money, as well as the farmers' produce, he argued, should be taken to carry on the war. In closing he said, "The agriculturists are not a favored class; there are no exempts among them; they have been the great sufferers in this war, both in blood and in treasure."[84]

Brown's prophecy that the farmers would be alienated from the cause was soon fulfilled. Later when he and Davis appealed to the farmers to plant corn, not one acre in fifty in the best corn district in Georgia was planted in corn.[85] Toombs planted a full crop of cotton and declared on every convenient occasion that "he, personally, would plant as much cotton as he pleased regardless of laws and vigilance committees."[86] The statements and conduct of such prominent men did not tend to create loyalty to the Confederacy in Georgia or elsewhere.

Criticism of the Tax-in-Kind Law

The tax-in-kind law, which took one-tenth of the farmers' produce for the Confederate government,[87] was condemned by Toombs and others on the same ground that Toombs had condemned the impressment law.[88] Since this

[83] *Ibid.*, pp. 988, 989, 1023, 1066.
[84] *A. C.* (1863), pp. 207-8.
[85] *Ibid.*, pp. 209-10; Chesnut, *Diary from Dixie*, p. 180.
[86] Ulrich B. Phillips, *Life of Robert Toombs*, p. 247; Chesnut, *Diary*, p. 180.
[87] *O. R.*, ser. IV, vol. II, pp. 521-22.   [88] Phillips, *op. cit.*, pp. 246, 248.

was the first general tax that the poorer people of the South had ever been conscious of paying and since land and slaves were not directly taxed, the people considered it as further evidence that this was a "rich man's war and a poor man's fight."[89]

After the passage of the impressment and tax-in-kind laws, the Confederate government was never again to have the confidence and support of the South, but it was always to be regarded with suspicion by the extreme state rights men and by those who thought the burdens of war were unevenly and unfairly distributed.[90] The leaders of the peace movements used the criticism of the state authorities to stir up dissatisfaction and to start the cry of "the Constitution as it is and the Union as it was."[91]

Criticism of Suspension of Writ of Habeas Corpus by State Rights Men

The suspension of the writ of habeas corpus gave further cause for complaint and furnished another argument for the peace leaders and the disloyal to use in alienating the people from Jefferson Davis and the Confederate cause. It was not difficult to convince many people, when Davis asked for the suspension of the writ of habeas corpus, that he was aiming at absolute power. Alexander H. Stephens, who was chiefly concerned with the championship of state rights, became the bitterest opponent of the suspension of the writ. In 1862, when the writ was suspended for the first time, he was almost alone in his opposition;[92] but in 1864, when it was suspended the last time,[93] the opposition to the Confederacy's policies and the management of the war had become so bitter and the disloyalty in certain sections so pronounced

---

[89] Schwab, *Confederate States of America*, pp. 224-25; Stephenson, *op. cit.*, p. 91.
[90] *Ibid.*, pp. 90-91.
[91] Schwab, *op. cit.*, pp. 220-22; Stephenson, *op. cit.*, p. 170.
[92] Phillips, *op. cit.*, p. 246; O. R., ser. IV, vol. I, p. 954.
[93] *Ibid.*, p. 1075.

that he found many zealous supporters. On every convenient occasion Stephens pronounced on Davis and his policies criticism which did much toward discrediting the administration and increasing the disloyalty and dissatisfaction among the people. The government's policies, he said, were "unwise, unconstitutional and dangerous to liberty."[94]

Antagonism was further aroused by distressing stories told by prominent men who were trying to show the misuse of the suspension of the writ. One of the stock stories concerned a soldier, who, marching by his home, stopped in to see his dying wife. When he returned to the ranks to get permission to bury her, he was shot as a deserter.[95]

Prevalence of Suffering

Another cause for the growth of disaffection and the formation of disloyal bands and peace societies was the suffering which came as a result of the war. Great privations were endured by all classes. The blockade had deprived the people not only of such luxuries as tea and coffee but also of such necessities as medicine, a hardship which remained throughout the war a distressing feature of southern life.[96] By 1863 food had become very scarce in many sections, partly because of the desolation by war of some of the most productive portions of the country and the reduction of the number of farmers by conscription, and partly because, although food was plentiful in some sections, the absence of any proper medium of exchange and the inadequate system of transportation prevented a proper distribution.[97] Heartless speculators hoarded supplies, and prices rose so much that many people could not buy.[98] Because of

[94] Schwab, *op. cit.*, p. 188.   [95] Stephenson, *op. cit.*, p. 85.
[96] *A. C.* (1863), pp. 6, 7, 211-12; Stephenson, *op. cit.*, p. 105; DeLeon, *op. cit.*, p. 186; Pryor, *Reminiscences of Peace and War*, pp. 239, 293; Schwab, *op. cit.*, p. 181.
[97] Pryor, *op. cit.*, p. 267; Stephenson, *op. cit.*, p. 108; *O. R.*, ser. IV, vol. II, pp. 158-59; *A. C.* (1863), p. 211.
[98] *O. R.*, ser. IV, vol. II, pp. 214, 901-2, 85-86; vol. I, pp. 250, 252, 253; *A. C.* (1863), pp. 211-12.

the depreciation of currency and the advance in prices[99] it was commonly said that one carried his money to market in a basket and brought his purchase home in his purse.[100] Everywhere the condition of the soldier's family became a tragedy, unless he was a landowner—many times even then—because his pay, regardless of his rank, was inadequate to provide for his dependents.[101] The soldier knew that the only thing which prevented his family from starving was the help given them by the state and county boards, by relief associations, or by their neighbors, who, too often, were in as serious a condition as they.[102] As early as 1863 in North Carolina, Alabama, Texas, Virginia, and other places, women and children raided stores to obtain food.[103]

As the Confederate lines were pushed back, many families fled from their homes to places of safety.[104] In the section occupied by the Federal armies the suffering of the people was further increased by the pillaging of the soldiers.[105] After the fall of Vicksburg Grant's soldiers were encouraged to live off the country and save their own supplies for an emergency.[106] The suffering of the people as a result of Sherman's march to the sea is too well known to need further description. After the fall of Vicksburg, the Southwest was practically isolated, and Mississippi and Alabama especially were exposed to the raids of the North, which swept the country clean of supplies. Huntsville, Alabama,

---

[99] Schwab, *op. cit.*, p. 181; O. R., ser. IV, vol. I, p. 739; A. C. (1863), pp. 211-12, 829; Pryor, *op. cit.*, p. 293; Jones, *Diary*, I, 261; *Eastern Clarion*, November 24, 1862, May 2, 1862, published at Paulding, Mississippi; *Natchez Courier*, April 10, 1862; *Weekly Mississippian*, November 19, 1861, and March 5, 1862.

[100] Chesnut, *Diary*, p. 284.

[101] DeLeon, *op. cit.*, p. 186; O. R., ser. IV, vol. I, pp. 130, 739.

[102] A. C. (1863), p. 447; Stephenson, *op. cit.*, pp. 109-10; *Eastern Clarion*, March 28, 1862.

[103] Pryor, *op. cit.*, pp. 237-39; A. C. (1863), pp. 6, 211, 818.

[104] Stephenson, *op. cit.*, p. 110.

[105] O. R., ser. I, vol. LII, pt. II, p. 312; vol. XXIII, pt. I, p. 245; vol. X, pt. II, p. 204.

[106] Pryor, *op. cit.*, p. 246.

which became a seat of disaffection during the war, had been raided twenty-one times before the close of 1863.[107]

Since the Southwest was left practically unprotected but was called on to furnish both men and supplies, it was only natural that the ardor of the people for the Confederacy should be lessened. Neither is it strange that many a soldier, either knowing or, what was worse, not knowing but imagining the suffering of his loved ones at home, slipped away from the army in the friendly darkness of the night and returned home. As will be noted later, many of these, to prevent capture and return to the army, formed into bands or joined a peace organization.

[107] Stephenson, *op. cit.*, pp. 118-19.

CHAPTER II
THE DEVELOPMENT OF PEACE SOCIETIES

BESIDES numerous organized bands that were to be found scattered throughout the Confederacy, three well developed disloyal peace societies, to which reference has been made in the preceding chapter, were organized during the Civil War and operated over large blocks of the Confederate States. These organizations were as follows: The Peace and Constitutional Society in Arkansas; the Peace Society, which honeycombed Alabama and extended into Georgia, Mississippi, and probably Florida; and the Order of the Heroes of America, which was found in North Carolina, East Tennessee, and Southwest Virginia, and which probably extended into South Carolina.

THE PEACE AND CONSTITUTIONAL SOCIETY

The first well organized secret peace society in the Confederacy came to light in Van Buren County, Arkansas, in the fall of 1861. It was called the Peace and Constitutional Society and was formed by men of Arkansas who had not favored leaving the Union in 1861 and who refused to support the Confederacy. Adjutant General Edmund Burgevin[1] reported its existence and the names of several men who, he thought, were connected with it. On October 29, 1861, twenty-seven of these men were arrested and sent to Little Rock to await trial by the civil authorities. A few days later others were arrested. Upon investigation it was found that these men were members of a regular organization known as the Peace and Constitutional Society, which

[1] David Y. Thomas, *Arkansas in War and Reconstruction, 1861-1874*, p. 84.

had been organized by the unionists[2] to oppose the Confederacy; that the society had about seven hundred members in Van Buren, Newton, and Izard counties, and about seventeen hundred members in the whole state. The order had signs, passwords, and an oath, and was receiving a regular supply of money. Each member was sworn to aid any member in distress, to encourage desertion from the Confederate army, to advocate joining the Federal army, and to support it when it came into Arkansas. The penalty for disclosing any of the secrets of the organization was death. The members who were arrested were well supplied with arms, and other members were said to have been equally well equipped.[3]

Most of the members lived in the northwestern part of the state in the hill counties, the section which, as already noted, was almost solidly against secession.[4]

The Peace Society

A far more potent and pernicious peace society than the Peace and Constitutional Society in Arkansas was the one known as the Peace Society, which existed in Alabama, East Tennessee, Georgia, Mississippi, and, perhaps, Florida.[5] Although the passwords, the grip, and the signs of this organization differed in various sections, the purposes of the order were everywhere practically the same. The first information concerning its existence was forwarded to Richmond in 1862 while Thomas H. Watts, later governor of Alabama, was a member of the Confederate Cabinet. At

---
[2] The term "unionist" here and elsewhere is used to mean those who opposed seceding in 1861. Some unionists did not believe in the right of secession while others did not believe there was sufficient cause to exercise the right of secession in 1861.
[3] *A. C.* (1861), p. 25; *O. R.*, ser. I, vol. VIII, p. 699.
[4] Bishop, *Loyalty on the Frontier*, pp. 21, 143-44.
[5] *O. R.*, ser. I, vol. VIII, pp. 699, 700-1.

his suggestion some of the Alabama troops that had been contaminated by it were sent to the front.[6]

The Peace Society probably originated in 1862 in North Alabama or East Tennessee within the Federal lines, at the suggestion of the Federals. It seems to have been introduced into the Confederate army at Cumberland Gap.[7] When discovered in December, 1863, in Clanton's brigade in South Alabama, it had among its members some men who had been members of another secret organization—probably the Heroes of America—which had originated with the Federals and had been introduced into the southern army at Cumberland Gap.[8]

Not much was known about the Peace Society until the latter part of 1863. In that year the results of the August election in Alabama were such that the Confederate authorities became suspicious and investigations were made which led to the disclosure of the existence of the organization.[9] By November, 1863, the provost marshal reported the existence of a treasonable peace society between the lines in Alabama and Tennessee, which had as one of its objects the encouragement of desertion from the Confederate army. The details of the organization were later made known by a Confederate soldier who had learned of the organization while in prison at Knoxville. After escaping from prison he returned to his home in Blount County, Alabama, in which there were many deserters from the Confederate army and in which disloyalty was widespread.[10] To get information concerning the or-

[6] *Ibid.*, vol. XXVI, pt. II, p. 556.

[7] *Ibid.*, pp. 552, 556; Walter L. Fleming, "The Peace Movement in Alabama During the Civil War," *South Atlantic Quarterly*, II (April, 1903), 250.

[8] *O. R.*, ser. I, vol. XXVI, pt. II, pp. 548-49, 551, 552, 556; Fleming, "The Peace Movement in Alabama," *loc. cit.*, pp. 249, 250; Fleming, *Civil War and Reconstruction in Alabama*, pp. 139-41.

[9] *O. R.*, ser. IV, vol. II, p. 726; Fleming, *Civil War and Reconstruction in Alabama*, pp. 138-39; Fleming, "The Peace Movement in Alabama," *loc. cit.*, p. 248.

[10] *O. R.*, ser. I, vol. XXXII, pt. III, pp. 681-82; Fleming, "The Peace Movement in Alabama," *loc. cit.*, p. 251. Private E. D. Meroney, Company D, Third Confed-

ganization, he joined it. He learned that the members were sworn not to give aid or comfort to a Confederate soldier, to an enrolling officer, or to anyone connected with the Conscription Bureau. Members were forbidden to write any of the secrets or signs of the order on anything. The signs of recognition were:

"1, Salute with the right hand closed, thumb pointing back behind the shoulder; 2, If the person saluted was one of the faithful, he would then grasp his own left hand with his right, knuckles of left hand down, of right hand up; 3, Both then looked one another in the eyes and each tapped his right foot with a stick; 4, One of them broke a small stick or like article and threw the pieces carelessly over the left shoulder. This mummery proved each to be faithful and signified that it was safe to speak of the secrets at that time and place; 5, In a crowd three careless slaps on the right leg served as a sign of the initiated; 6, If in prison, the word 'Washington' four times repeated would secure release within twenty-four hours, if guarded by the faithful; 7, When halted or challenged by a federal picket or sentinel, the countersign was 'Jack'. The sentinel would then reply, 'All right, Jack, pass on with your goose quills'; 8, In battle the sign was made by placing the butt of the gun against the right hip and inclining the barrel at an angle of forty-five degrees to the right. After holding it in this position long enough to be noticed, the rifle was then carried to the position of left shoulder arms, according to Scott's regulations."[11]

This society maintained a line of communication between

erate Cavalry, was captured at Philadelphia, East Tennessee, on Oct. 20, 1863, and imprisoned at Knoxville. While there he learned of the Peace Society.—*O. R.* ser. I, vol. XXXII, pt. III, p. 681.

[11] *O. R.*, ser. I, vol. XXXII, pt. III, pp. 682-83; Fleming, "The Peace Movement in Alabama," *loc. cit.*, pp. 250-51.

the enemy in North Alabama and Tennessee as far south as Tallapoosa County.[12]

A few months later Colonel Jefferson Falkner of the Eighth Confederate Infantry discovered the existence of the Peace Society in Middle Alabama. Colonel Falkner was approached by W. C. Brown, Jr., and asked if he had any desire to know about an order which had for its object the bringing about of a speedy peace. When Colonel Falkner answered in the affirmative, Brown called one James Wood, who proceeded to initiate Falkner into the order.[13]

In order to learn more about the society, Colonel Falkner and A. R. Hill of Wedowee, Randolph County, induced Theophilus Burke, a citizen of Meriwether County, Georgia, to join the society. Burke was initiated into it in Randolph County by William Kent, an influential citizen of Randolph County, who was known to be disloyal to the Confederacy.[14] From Burke and others who made investigations, it was discovered that the objects of the order were as follows: to organize a political party opposed to the administration; to get a majority of the people at home and as many soldiers as possible committed to this party; to overturn the existing state government by beginning hostilities against the home guards and secessionists, or, by refusing to support the existing state government, to compel it to make peace; and, above all, to break down the Confederate government. Although the plans were not perfected, some were in favor of returning to the Union on the Arkansas or Sebastian platform as suggested by Colonel Seibels, while others wished to send to

[12] *O. R.*, ser. I, vol. XXXII, pt. III, p. 682; Fleming, "The Peace Movement in Alabama," *loc. cit.*, p. 251.

[13] *Ibid.*, ser. IV, vol. III, pp. 395-396; Fleming, "The Peace Movement in Alabama," *loc. cit.*, pp. 252-53.

[14] *O. R.*, ser. IV, vol. III, pp. 396-98; Fleming, "The Peace Movement in Alabama," *loc. cit.*, p. 253.

Washington to make terms, and still others were in favor of submitting unconditionally to the North.[15]

Although the society in the central counties was in communication with the Peace Society of North Alabama, the grips, passwords, and signals differed. The grip of the order in central Alabama was given by taking hold of the hand as usual in shaking hands, except that the thumb was turned with the side instead of the ball to the back of the hand. Then the following dialogue ensued:

"What is that?"
"A grip."
"A grip of what?"
"A constitutional peace grip."
"Has it a name?"
"It has."
"Will you give it to me?"
"I did not so receive it, neither can I so impart it."
"How will you impart it?"
"I will letter it with you."
"Letter it and begin."
"Begin you."
"No, you begin."
"Begin you."

Then the word "peace," which was the password, was spelled "by calling a letter alternately, beginning with any letter except the first." Various signs of recognition were used. The person giving the sign took up a stick, or some similar object, held it in both hands in front of the body and then carelessly threw it to the right using both hands. This sign was "recognized by putting the right hand to the lock of

[15] *O. R.*, ser. IV, vol. III, pp. 396, 397; Nicolay and Hay, *Abraham Lincoln*, VIII, 410-15; Fleming, *Civil War and Reconstruction in Alabama*, p. 142. The Arkansas or Sebastian platform was a plan suggested by E. W. Gantt, William Fishback, and others for the return of Arkansas to the Union. It was merely a plan to have the people instruct W. K. Sebastian, former United States senator from Arkansas, whose term had not expired, to return to his seat in the United States Senate.

the hair on the right side of the head as if pulling off something and throwing it to the right." Another sign consisted "in tapping three times on the toe of the right foot with a switch or stick, and then waving it to the right. Another sign consists in taking a switch, stick, or whip and setting it on the right thigh and then leaning it to the right"; or, if the person giving the sign was an officer, he carried "his sword with the point inclined to the right, and if on horseback, with the hilt resting on the thigh." The soldier on the battle field gave the sign by "carrying his gun with the muzzle inclined to the right." The sign of distress was given "by extending the right hand horizontally and then bringing it down by three distinct motions"; or, if this sign could not be given, the words, "Oh! Washington!" were substituted for it. The expression "I dreamed that the boys are all coming home" was also used as a means of recognition.[16]

When a man was taken into the society, he was asked if he were a constitutional man, to which he was expected to answer yes. Then he was told he would be required to take an oath or obligation which would not conflict with his political or religious principles. The candidate was then required to swear that he would never reveal or make known any of the secrets of the order to anyone, except to a brother of the order, and not to him until after "strict trial and lawful information" as to his standing; that he would never "cut, carve, mark, scratch, chop, &c., upon anything, movable or immovable, under the whole canopy of heaven, whereby any of the secrets of this order might become legible or intelligible"; that he would not impart any of the secrets of the order "to an old man in his dotage, to a young man in his nonage, to a woman, or to a fool"; that he would always aid a brother of the order and would rush to his relief at the

---

[16] *O. R.*, ser. IV, vol. III, p. 397; Fleming, "The Peace Movement in Alabama," *loc. cit.*, p. 254.

sign of distress—even feign to be his enemy if necessary, in order to assist him; that he would aid his brother's widow and children when appealed to; and that he would not wrong a brother of the order nor suffer it to be done by others if it were in his power to prevent it. To all this the candidate was pledged under the following oath: "I bind myself under no less penalty than that of having my head cut open, my brains taken from thence and strewn over the ground, my body cast to the beasts of the field or to the vultures of the air should I be so vile as to reveal any of the secrets of this order."[17]

The strength of the Peace Society lay in Alabama and Georgia. Men well versed in all of the signs, passwords, grips, and purposes of the order were known as "eminents" and travelled over the country giving the "degree" to all whom they considered fit subjects. The eminents did not always make known all of the secrets to every member. If the man initiated was ignorant but loyal, he was told that the object of the order was to procure an honorable peace; if disaffected as to the policy of the administration, he was told that the aim was to procure a change of rulers; if a traitor, he was told that the aim was to produce mutiny among the soldiers, destroy the loyal citizens of the Confederate States, work against the Confederacy, and take Alabama back into the Union on any terms. The Peace Society, as the order was called unless an eminent saw fit to give it some particular name for the occasion, kept no records, had no regular times or places of meeting, and had no organized "lodges" or "communities." Since each member was "an independent, dissevered link in a perfect chain," being told by an eminent who his associates or brethren were, it was very difficult to deal with the order. It was, the report stated, "a society without officers, a community without members." One man

[17] O. R., ser. IV, vol. III, p. 395; Fleming, "The Peace Movement in Alabama," *loc. cit.*, p. 253.

could be proved to be a member, but outside of his statements there was no other proof of other memberships. It was extremely difficult to get evidence against the members who were believed to be disloyal. The charge had to be proved against one man at a time, because few had firsthand knowledge of the acts of others.[18]

Although some of the members of the Peace Society did not mean to be disloyal to the Confederacy, the order was a dangerous instrument in the hands of disloyal and designing politicians, and did much harm, as will be noted later.

Order of the Heroes of America

A third well developed disloyal organization in the Confederacy was that of the Order of the Heroes of America, which became very potent and pernicious in North Carolina, southwestern Virginia, and eastern Tennessee.[19] This organization was not discovered until 1864; but early in the war disaffection and treason were manifested in the sections in which the Order was later discovered; and since the disloyal were carrying out what was later found to be the purposes of the society, it no doubt had been organized early in the war. Exactly when, where, and by whom this society was first started remains a question. Some say it was organized in North Carolina by Union sympathizers. The *Raleigh Standard* said that Henderson Adams, the state auditor in Governor W. W. Holden's administration, was one of its founders.[20] Brigadier General John Echols, who in 1864 was aiding in ferreting out the members of the society in southwestern Virginia, reported to Secretary Seddon that the organization had existed there for many months; that it had been "formed originally at the suggestion of the Yankee

---

[18] *O. R.*, ser. IV., vol. III, pp. 393-94. Fleming, "The Peace Movement in Alabama," *loc. cit.*, p. 256.

[19] *O. R.*, ser. IV, vol. III, pp. 813-15.

[20] J. G. DeRoulhac Hamilton, "Heroes of America," *Publications of the Southern Historical Association*, XI (January, 1907), 10.

authorities"; and that the order also existed in East Tennessee and North Carolina.[21] Both Echols and N. F. Bocock, who was also sent out by Secretary Seddon to aid in the investigation of the society, reported that the organization had its headquarters within the Federal lines.[22] Henry Questine, a member of the society in Montgomery County, Virginia, said that the order there had been organized in the fall of 1863 by Horace Dean, of North Carolina, when he passed through Virginia on his way home from Richmond.[23] In the early part of December, 1861, Brigadier General W. H. Carroll informed General A. S. Johnston that an effort was on foot for a thorough organization of the disloyal in East Tennessee and the border counties of North Carolina.[24] Whether the Federals had anything to do with originating the society or not, the Federal officers were well informed as to the character and purpose of the order and allowed its members to pass freely through their lines. As an inducement to join the society, the Federals offered its members "exemption from military service; protection to their persons and property during the war; and, at the conclusion thereof, participation in the division of the real estate of the loyal [Confederate] citizens." The latter promise was emphasized among the ignorant mountaineers.[25] The fact that both Lincoln and Grant were members of the organization gave all the more color to such a promise.[26]

The Order of the Heroes of America had a grip, passwords, signs, obligations, and an oath which every member was required to take. The passwords ordinarily consisted of the following questions and answers:

Question: These are gloomy times.

[21] *O. R.*, ser. IV, vol. III, pp. 813-14.
[22] *Ibid.*, pp. 803, 814.
[23] *Ibid.*, p. 807.
[24] *O. R.*, ser. I, vol. LII, pt. II, p. 232.
[25] *O. R.*, ser. IV, vol. III, pp. 814-15.
[26] Testimony of Daniel R. Goodloe (a former U. S. marshal of Warren County), *Senate Report*, 1st sess., 42nd Congress, ser. 1468, p. 227.

Answer: Yes, but we are looking for better.
Question: What are you looking for?
Answer: A red and white cord.
Question: Why a cord?
Answer: Because it is safe for us and our families.[27]

Occasionally when a person was not suspected of being a spy, these passwords were dispensed with. After the grip and the signs had been given, one person would say "Three." If the other answered "Days," that was considered sufficient evidence that the men were brothers of the order.[28]

Every person upon being admitted into the society was required to take an oath to perform faithfully the duties imposed upon its members and to swear on penalty of death not to divulge its secrets.[29] The duties required were to encourage and facilitate desertion from the Confederate army, to protect and pass all deserters, escaped prisoners, or spies; to report the positions, movements, numbers, and condition of the Confederate troops; in short, to contribute in every way possible to the success of the Federals and the defeat of the Confederacy.[30]

It will be recalled that in East Tennessee not only had most of the people opposed leaving the Union, but also East Tennessee had attempted to separate from the rest of the state when Tennessee seceded; that in Southwest Virginia not more than one-fourth of the people had favored secession; and that in North Carolina there was strong opposition to secession until Lincoln called for the state's quota of troops to help coerce the seceding states. In the mountainous sections of these three states, there were many men who were not in any way concerned with the questions before the people. They caused no trouble until a conscription act was passed and the apathetic mountaineers and unionists were

---

[27] O. R., ser. IV, vol. III, pp. 806, 809, 811.
[28] O. R., ser. IV, vol. III, p. 810.
[29] *Ibid.*, p. 814.   [30] *Ibid.*, pp. 803, 807, 814.

called upon to leave their families unprotected and uncared for and to endure the hardships and privations of the army to fight for the Confederacy, for which they had no love. The result was that many of them resorted to every possible means of keeping out of the army; and, if these failed, they deserted at the first opportunity. It was these, their families, and others who opposed the war for various reasons, who became members of the disloyal peace organizations.

In addition to these three well organized societies, there were many disloyal bands to be found in the swamps of Florida, Georgia, Alabama, and Mississippi; in the hilly and mountainous sections of the Confederacy; and among the Germans in Texas. These various organizations were made up of persons who, for one reason or another, refused to fight for the Confederacy. A few bands, no doubt, were organized solely for plunder. A common purpose of all of them, however, was to escape service in the army.

Although there was no close connection among the well developed peace organizations and the many scattered disloyal bands which honeycombed the Confederacy, yet when the disloyal men of the Confederacy passed from one section to another, they had no difficulty in obtaining protection from the treasonable organization which existed in that particular community, and they could easily become affiliated with such organization if they so desired.

In the following chapters the operation of all these organizations in the various states of the Confederacy will be discussed.

CHAPTER III
DISAFFECTION WEST OF THE MISSISSIPPI

The Peace and Constitutional Society in Arkansas

Opposition to the Confederacy existed in Arkansas from the beginning, and, as has already been noted, the first secret peace society in the Confederacy came to light in that state. During November and December of 1861, many men from counties both north and south of the Arkansas River were arrested for belonging to the Peace and Constitutional Society. Governor Rector appealed to President Davis and Secretary of War Judah P. Benjamin for instructions to guide him in dealing with the members of this treasonable organization. On November 28 he wrote Davis that he was still holding the twenty-seven men who had been sent to Little Rock on October 29 because they were suspected of being members of the Peace and Constitutional Society, and that he expected a hundred more in a day or so. He said, too, writing to Benjamin on December 3, that sixty-four from Searcy County and forty-seven from Izard County had been arrested, but that the citizens had permitted them to volunteer and had asked the state authorities to sanction their course. Some of the men had been sent to General McCulloch and the others to Colonel Borland, stationed at Pocahontas. Since Governor Rector believed that the disloyal men, if allowed to enter the army, should be sent south, where they would be removed from the influences of home and of disloyal associates, he refused to sanction the course of the citizens unless it were first approved by the Confederate administration.[1] The Secretary of War replied that, at that distance and with imperfect knowledge of the facts,

[1] *O. R.*, ser. I, vol. VIII, pp. 699, 700-1.

it was impossible for him to say what should be done with the members of the society who had been arrested, and he advised the Governor to use his best judgment in acting on the information before him.[2]

In the meantime, conditions in Izard and some other counties had become so alarming that Colonel Solon Borland had sent two companies of infantry to aid in suppressing the disloyal movement; but by the time they arrived the loyal citizens, who had organized into Home Guards for their own protection, had captured the disloyal men, and Borland's men had nothing to do but collect the prisoners who had been captured or who had voluntarily surrendered. About forty of the prisoners were sent to Little Rock; seventy-five or eighty were confined in the jails of different counties; and fifty-seven were taken to Colonel Borland. Many of these ignorant men, claiming they had been misled by others who had made their escape from the country, begged to be allowed to take the oath of allegiance to the Confederacy and to enter one of Borland's companies. Because of the stigma attached to disloyalty, none of them wished to return home. Without consulting anyone, Borland decided that since they had not yet committed any overt act of disloyalty to the Confederacy, he would enroll as soldiers all of those fit for military service and keep the others for teamsters and mechanics. On December 11 he informed General A. S. Johnston of his actions and requested him to approve his course.[3]

In accordance with the pledge to the Peace and Constitutional Society, men who became members of the organization soon began to join the Union army. In December one member of the legislature and forty other men joined the Federals at Rollo, Missouri, and reported to them that there was much Union sentiment in the northern part of Arkansas.[4]

[2] *Ibid.*, p. 702.
[3] *Ibid.*, pp. 709-10.
[4] *A. C.* (1861), p. 25.

When Governor Rector had delivered his message to the legislature, on the first Monday in November, he had alluded to "the existence of 'treason in the state'" but did not give any of the details concerning it since they were already well known.[5]

In view of the bitter opposition to secession and the strong Union sentiment existing in Northwest Arkansas, it is not surprising to find the Unionists organizing not only against the Confederacy but also for self-protection. While the question of secession was being considered, both the secessionists and unionists had tried to create public sentiment in their favor, and after the war began they continued their efforts. The Germans and the Irish never showed any inclination to enlist in the Confederate army.[6] The secessionists attempted to rally the people to the support of the Confederacy by declaring that its failure would bring Negro equality, which would inevitably result in trouble with the Negroes. This statement took on increased significance in June, 1861, when a plot was unearthed among the Negroes in Monroe County to murder all the white men and, in case they offered any resistance, the women and children. Several Negroes were arrested on the charge of attempting to start this insurrection, and three—two men and one girl —were hanged. Although the fear of Negro equality caused some of the more ignorant to rally to the support of the Confederacy, the better educated natives and the foreign-born Irish and Germans were not disturbed by this prediction and continued to refuse to give their support.[7]

During 1862 the attempt to enforce the conscription law, the occupation of northern Arkansas by the Federals,

---

[5] *Ibid.*

[6] Bishop, *Loyalty on the Frontier*, pp. 20-21, 22, 141, 143-44, 148, 181; *A. C.* (1861), p. 25. In 1860 there were 1,312 Irish and 1,143 Germans in Arkansas. —Thomas, *op. cit.*, p. 12.

[7] *A. C.* (1861), p. 25; Bishop, *op. cit.*, pp. 9-10.

and the failure of the Confederacy to give aid to Arkansas aroused hostility and increased the disloyalty to the Confederacy. When the conscription law was passed, men realized that unless exemption could be secured, they must either enroll for Confederate service or flee; and many chose to do the latter.[8] Some went to the hills and others joined the Federals. Many of those who took their families went to Cassville, Missouri. Most of the unionists who wished to enlist in the Federal army went to Springfield, Missouri. Various schemes were used by the Federals to induce all who came to enter the army. Practically all of the officers advised them to enlist and go back to Arkansas to protect their homes and take vengeance on their enemies. Many followed this advice. The First Arkansas Cavalry, in which A. W. Bishop, an ardent Arkansas unionist, was an officer, was made up mostly of Union men from Arkansas who joined the Federals at Springfield, Missouri, with the avowed purpose of returning to their communities to arouse the disaffected, protect their homes, and take vengeance on their persecutors. Charles Galloway, a staunch Union man from Banny County, who had bitterly opposed secession, raised two companies in Stone County, brought them to Springfield to enlist in the Union army, and then returned home with them to fight. In some cases Federal officers compelled the refugees to enlist by ordering that no food be given to anyone who did not enlist.[9]

When the Federals took possession of Northwest Arkansas in the early part of the year, the disloyal flocked to

[8] Suddenly vocations which secured exemptions became very popular. Teachers paid pupils to come to them; from $50 to $500 were offered for positions in post offices; some men became salt makers, while others received a sudden call to the ministry. Further complaint was caused as a result of many of the exempts engaging in speculation. Trading with the enemy was very lucrative.—Thomas, *op. cit.*, pp. 98, 99, 100.

[9] Bishop, *op. cit.*, pp. 11-13, 27-28, 200-1, 202-3; O. R., ser. I, vol. XIII, pp. 444-45; Thomas, *op. cit.*, pp. 382-83. *See below*, pp. 41-42.

them for protection and the Federal officers continued to encourage them in enlisting and to nurture the Union sentiment in the state.[10] Since the Richmond government could give Arkansas no aid, much dissatisfaction was aroused among the citizens loyal to the Confederacy who criticized Davis and his policies. This naturally tended to encourage the disloyal. No one was more indignant at this lack of support by the Confederate administration than was Governor Rector and in an address which he issued to the people in May, he furnished the unionists and other disaffected elements with a new argument to arouse hostility to the Confederacy. In this address he said:

> It was for liberty that Arkansas struck, and not for subordination to any created secondary power, north or south. . . . If the arteries of the Confederate heart do not permeate beyond the east bank of the Mississippi, let southern Missourians, Arkansians, Texans and the great West know it and prepare for the future. Arkansas lost, abandoned, subjugated, is not Arkansas as she entered the Confederate Government. Nor will she remain Arkansas, a Confederate State, desolated as a wilderness. Her children, fleeing from the wrath to come, will build them a new ark, and launch it on new waters, seeking a haven somewhere of equality, safety, and rest.[11]

Members of the Peace and Constitutional Society were in constant communication with the Federals, and reports of Federal officers tend to reveal the state of feeling against the Confederacy and the aid given to the Federals. On February 23, 1862, the Federal commander at Fayetteville reported that the unionists were begging him to remain and that they promised to furnish food for his men and forage for his animals if he would stay. Believing that the Union families would go with his army if it moved, he suggested

---

[10] *O. R.*, ser. I, vol. VIII, pp. 69-70; vol. XIII, p. 452; *A. C.* (1862), pp. 11, 55; Bishop, *op. cit.*, p. 203.

[11] *A. C.* (1862), p. 11.

that he be allowed to remain at Fayetteville.¹² On April 5 General Samuel R. Curtis reported to Halleck that West Arkansas, which never had "much real affection" for the rebellion was "particularly sick of [it]";¹³ and a month later, from his camp at Batesville, he reported that the Union sentiment in the state was strong "and in town considerable," that, in fact, the people seemed ready to abandon the Confederacy. The demonstration of joy with which he was received and the later acts of the people certainly justified him in making such a report. Judges, clergymen, and other influential citizens took the oath of allegiance to the United States, and many meetings were held in which resolutions pledging unconditional support to the Union were adopted. At Reeves' Station a committee was sent to meet and welcome General Steele and his men. Other reports show that the Union sentiment in the state was increasing and that many were ready and anxious to abandon the Confederacy.¹⁴

On June 22 the Federal officer, General E. B. Brown, wrote General Schofield that William Fishback, a lawyer from Fort Smith, had left Springfield that morning for St. Louis and would call on General Schofield upon arriving. Brown said Fishback had reported to him that the enforcement of the conscription law, which began on June 20, was "making Union people fast"; that between four thousand and five thousand men could be armed against the Confederacy in the western part of Arkansas. From him and others, Brown said, "I learn[ed] that all the regular forces of the enemy have been moved to Little Rock. A few irregular troops have possession of West Arkansas. [This] confirms the report of [a] line of scouts to prevent the people leaving."¹⁵ Refugees from Arkansas, Brown reported,

¹² Report of Brigadier General Asboth of the Second Division, *O. R.*, ser. I, vol. VIII, p. 69.
¹³ *O. R.*, ser. I, vol. VIII, p. 662.
¹⁴ *Ibid.*, vol. XIII, pp. 365, 369, 373, 444-45; *A. C.* (1862), p. 11.
¹⁵ *O. R.*, ser. I, vol. XIII, p. 444.

were coming to all of the Federal posts; twenty came to Forsyth and showed a white flag; seventeen had appeared at Springfield, had enlisted, and had asked to be sent back to Arkansas to fight. To compel all refugees to enlist, General Brown ordered that no food be given to anyone who did not enlist.

On August 17, 1862, Brown again wrote Schofield: "A secret agent of a Union Organization visited me yesterday, with a view to arranging some way by which a large number of Arkansas citizens could escape."[16] Although these citizens lived south of the Arkansas River, Brown said, they were willing to cross the mountains if the Federals would meet them. A regiment of unionists had been raised and partly armed, but because of the indiscretion of some of its officers, the plot was discovered and all of the regiment captured by the Confederates. About two hundred of the men were imprisoned. Brown further reported that the conscripts from north of the mountains had been taken by the Confederates to Fort Smith, where they were being drilled; but, because so many of them were Union men, they were not trusted with arms.[17]

In order to deal with the members of the Peace and Constitutional Society and other disloyal people in the state, the General Assembly in November, 1862, passed a law making the giving of comfort and aid to the enemy an offense punishable by death; but it was scouted and defied in Northwest Arkansas.[18]

By 1863 the disaffection had increased, and the presence of the Federals in the state made the disloyal very bold. Large numbers of men deserted to the enemy. By July only one Confederate newspaper remained in the state. By December eight regiments, consisting of both whites and blacks, had enlisted in the Federal service. Life and property,

[16] *Ibid.*, p. 581.   [17] *Ibid.*, pp. 580, 581.
[18] Bishop, *op. cit.*, pp. 195-97, 194; Thomas, *op. cit.*, p. 101.

especially in North Arkansas, were insecure, and Union sympathizers fled to the Union army for protection while the Confederate sympathizers went south. By the fall of 1863 the Federals had captured Little Rock and had cleared the country northeast of the Arkansas River of organized Confederate soldiers—an accomplishment which encouraged many to advocate publicly a return to the Union.[19]

The active leaders in the reconstruction movement were a few true unionists and some men who had been in the Confederate service but had remained loyal to the South only so long as they thought that she was going to win and that loyalty to the Confederacy was good policy. William Fishback and E. W. Gantt were two of this latter type. In the beginning of the war Fishback had pretended to aid the Confederacy but, as has already been noted, he was in communication with the Federals as early as June, 1862; he had renewed his allegiance to the Union and was giving information intended to aid it and to injure the Confederacy. Later he deserted to the enemy, and in October, 1863, under the protection of the Federals at Little Rock, he addressed a large audience of Union sympathizers and urged them to return to the Union; in November, 1863, he began the work of organizing the Fourth Arkansas Cavalry Volunteers. Gantt, a former brigadier general in the Confederate army and once a prisoner of war, had also seen the error of his way; and he was found, in 1863, declaring in a public address: "The loyalty to Jeff. Davis in Arkansas does not extend practically beyond the shadow of his army, while the hatred of him is as widespread as it is intense. The Union sentiment is manifesting itself on all sides and by every indication—in Union meetings—in desertions from the Confederate army—in taking the oath of allegiance

---

[19] T. S. Staples, *Reconstruction in Arkansas*, pp. 10-11, 12, 13; *A. C.* (1863), p. 15; Thomas, *op. cit.*, pp. 382-90. From first to last 8,789 Arkansians joined the Federal forces but 1,025 deserted before the end of the war.—*Ibid.*, pp. 388-89.

[to the United States] unsolicited—in organizing for home defense, and enlisting in the Federal army." The little county of Perry, he said, which had only about six hundred voters and which had been "turned wrong side out in search of conscripts by Hindman and his fellow-murderers and oppressors, with their retinue of salaried gentlemen and negro boys," had sent a company of ninety-four men to the Union army.[20]

Gantt and Fishback both favored returning to the Union on what was later known as the Sebastian plan, which was merely a plan to have the people instruct W. K. Sebastian, former United States senator whose term had not expired, to return to his seat in the United States Senate. Union meetings were held in various places and other plans for reconstruction were offered. Numerous meetings were held, many of which were promoted and dominated by soldiers. From this time on, many came out boldly and advocated the Union cause, although the more timid continued to aid it secretly until the close of the war, because they feared the Confederates might return and wreak vengeance on them.[21]

Disaffection in Texas

In Texas there was much disaffection and active opposition to the Confederacy during the war. While there seems to have been no well developed, widespread peace societies such as existed in some of the other Confederate States, there were well organized bands composed of unionists, conscripts, deserters, and other disloyal people who openly defied the Confederate Government and endangered the lives and property of its adherents. After Texas seceded, many who had opposed withdrawing from the Union loyally supported the Confederacy; but some of those who

[20] *A. C.* (1863), p. 15; Thomas, *op. cit.*, pp. 384-85, 391, 394; Staples, *op. cit.*, pp. 12, 13, 16.

[21] Staples, *op. cit.*, pp. 13-21; *A. C.* (1863), p. 15; Thomas, *op. cit.*, p. 394.

had opposed secession went North, some joined the Federal army, and many others stayed, hiding at times in the woods and hills to evade the conscription officers, until at last they were forced to flee the country.[22] Many of the disaffected who remained at home and claimed loyalty to the new government gave it only a half-hearted support and increased the opposition to the Confederacy by criticizing Davis and his policy in conducting the war.[23]

The first open opposition was shown by unionists in the southwestern part of the state. On October 4, 1861, Colonel Charles Anderson, brother of Robert Anderson of Fort Sumter and leader of the Union opposition at San Antonio, was arrested.[24] On November 7, because of the strong Union sentiment at Carrizo in Dimmit County, bands organized and began to make raids on the loyal Confederates.[25] Four days later, it was reported that Mexicans in Zapata County, backed by a strong party in Guerrero across the line in Mexico, had not only refused allegiance to the Confederate States but had announced their "intention to take service with the North should Mr. Lincoln send an invading force to the Rio Grande." This group had already made raids on loyal citizens, and the Confederate authorities were warned that they might "do much mischief."[26]

When the conscription officers appeared, the Germans around Austin caused much trouble. They organized to resist conscription, openly rebelled against the Confederate government,[27] and endangered the lives and property of loyal citizens.[28] In August, 1862, about sixty unionists, most of whom were Germans, collected at Fredericksburg,

[22] Ramsdell, *Reconstruction in Texas*, p. 22.
[23] Rowland, *Jefferson Davis, Constitutionalist: His Letters, Papers, and Speeches*, V, 442-43.
[24] *O. R.*, ser. I, vol. IV, p. 115.
[25] *Ibid.*, pp. 131-32. [26] *Ibid.*, p. 137.
[27] *Ibid.*, vol. XV, pp. 925, 926, 927, 929, 936.
[28] *Ibid.*, vol. XXVI, pt. II, p. 236.

about thirty-five miles west of Austin. They decided to go to New Orleans by way of Mexico to join the Federals; but they were attacked by the Confederates, who killed about two-thirds of their number.[29] In November, 1862, the enrolling officer for Austin County reported to the superintendent of conscripts at Austin that the Germans in that region not only were evading the conscription law but also were holding secret meetings, in which they were planning resistance. From four hundred to five hundred persons usually attended these secret meetings. They also held one public meeting, in which they petitioned the governor to provide for their families and to arm and clothe the conscripts as a preliminary to their submission to the conscription law and their entrance into the Confederate service. The enrolling officer asked for a mounted and well armed force to bring the conscripts in. The militia could not be depended upon to enforce the law because nearly all of its force sympathized with the disloyal conscripts.[30]

On December 23 a draft in response to the Governor's proclamation calling for men was held at Industry, in Austin County, and a number were drafted; but they refused to be sworn into the state service. So incensed were the disloyal who had been drafted that on the day appointed by the captain stationed at Industry for them to appear and be sworn into service, they had appeared, but only to assault the captain and to drive him away from the appointed place, and to mob and beat a friend of his with sticks and iron bars. It

[29] Rev. John H. Aughey, *Tupelo*, p. 558. Rev. Mr. Aughey was a Presbyterian minister who was born in New York but had labored in Mississippi for eleven years preceding the Civil War. Most of this time had been spent in the central and northeast part of the state. He was a staunch unionist and was imprisoned in 1862 at Tupelo because of his outspoken sympathy for the Union and his opposition to the Confederacy. After escaping from prison, he became a chaplain in the United States Army. While in Mississippi, he headed the unionist organization in Tishomingo County. He describes the work of the unionists in Northeast Mississippi and their persecution by the Confederates.

[30] *O. R.*, ser. I, vol. XV, p. 887.

was these disloyal men and the conscripts who joined them that called for a meeting to plan some definite action to protect themselves.[31]

On December 31, 1862, this meeting, called to decide on a concerted plan of action, convened in the upper part of Austin County. About six hundred men were present, including regularly appointed delegates from Austin, Washington, Fayette, Lavaca, and Colorado counties. It was decided that "one man in each beat" should return home, call his men together, organize them into companies of infantry and cavalry, and also keep "a picket guard mounted and armed, to be ready to communicate information to the officers in command." Many of them had already been drilling regularly. At this meeting speeches were made by the following: Fr. Mittanck, F. Honbold, H. Zulauf, F. W. Dorbritz, and C. Rungo, of New Ulm, Austin County; one Sulinger, and Helams, Sr., also of Austin County; and A. M. Hildebrand and Lewis of Fayette County. Lewis was not a German. Every speaker urged resistance to the Confederate government and opposed going into service either for the Confederate or the state government.[32]

On January 4, 1863, General Webb reported that between five hundred and seven hundred men, representing six counties, had held a meeting in Austin County. Some loyal men, who attended the meeting, said that plans were made to assemble and resist the state draft and the Confederate conscription laws when the men were ordered out; and that plans were also made "to stir up insurrection with all of its horrors in case of conflict." Both Germans and Americans addressed the meeting.[33]

Many other meetings of a similar character were re-

[31] *Ibid.*, p. 926.
[32] *Ibid.*, pp. 925-29. The state government had drafted some men for service but these speakers urged resistance to any kind of army service.
[33] *Ibid.*, pp. 926-27.

ported. As a result of these meetings, the disloyal began to collect arms and threatened with destruction every German who would not join them. A German secessionist "was kicked out of one of the meetings . . . and charged with being a spy."[34] At this time a German blacksmith was caught making spearheads to be used in case an insurrection was thought necessary.

Webb was convinced that the seeds of disloyalty had been sown by American traitors who were working among the Germans and urging them to resist. In fact, he believed most of the Germans would have remained loyal had it not been for native American traitors. But this is probably not true, because the German people were not only more in sympathy with the ideals of the United States than they were with those of the Confederacy but they did not wish to leave their families and fight. Moreover, because of the violent threats made by some of the Germans who were led by Americans, many that otherwise would perhaps have been loyal to the Confederacy were afraid to enter the army and leave their families unprotected. Webb believed that the greatest disaffection in that section was in Austin and Fayette counties.[35] Without question there was much disloyalty in both. On January 4, 1863, about one hundred twenty citizens in Biegel Settlement in Fayette County held a meeting and drew up a declaration which expressed their sentiment and sent it to Webb. The substance of the declaration was as follows: the soldiers' families were not cared for; the soldiers' pay was insufficient to provide for their families; they were not interested in the principles for which the war was being waged; they declined to take the army oath to the Confederate States; and, therefore, they would not be able to answer the call for service.[36]

The next day a regiment was sent to Alleyton, and from

[34] *Ibid.*, p. 927.
[35] *Ibid.*, pp. 927, 928.
[36] *Ibid.*, pp. 928-29.

there forces were sent out to disarm the Germans and enforce the draft and conscription acts.[37] A few days later General Magruder found it necessary to send several companies and a piece of artillery to Colorado County to aid in suppressing about eight hundred Germans who were well armed and who had gathered to resist the military laws of the Confederacy.[38]

Early in January, 1863, Governor Flanagin met a committee representing the one hundred twenty men who had held the meeting at Biegel Settlement and who had signed the declaration giving their reasons for being unable to answer any call to service. He gave them a "very plain, positive talk," which Webb believed would result in the drafted men's enrolling at the specified time.[39]

Commissions of loyal and influential citizens were then sent by Webb to all the disaffected regions to appeal to the people to do their duty. Webb again reported that some Americans were urging the Germans to resist. Nevertheless, it was believed that most of the men would appear on the appointed day, though some of them declared that at the first opportunity after they entered the service "they would hoist the white flag and go over to the enemy."[40]

Ex-Governor Sam Houston gave encouragement to the disloyal bands by criticizing Davis. In March, 1863, Guy M. Bryan, of Waco, Texas, wrote President Davis that Houston, who was thinking of running for governor, was taking advantage of the growing feeling of dissatisfaction among the people at what they considered "unwarranted exercise of powers by the military authorities," and was inculcating the idea that Davis was responsible for "the offensive acts of the military." Houston, he said, referred to the president as "Jeffy Davis" who "desired to be made em-

[37] *Ibid.*, p. 931.
[38] *Ibid.*, p. 936.   [39] *Ibid.*, p. 945.   [40] *Ibid.*

peror." If Houston were elected, Bryan feared that Texas would be lost to the Confederacy.[41]

There was also considerable disaffection in the counties south of the Red River and in other sections of the state. General E. Kirby Smith reported in October, 1863, that affairs around Bonham, in Fannin County, and in other parts of the state had reached such a crisis that "the question is whether they or we shall control." He suggested arresting and sending the leaders of the disloyal beyond the Rio Grande and then winning back or exterminating the deserters.[42] General McCulloch received many letters from various districts asking him to arrest deserters and conscripts who had gone into the brush and were living on the produce of the loyal citizens and endangering their lives.[43] The question of desertion in Texas continued to be a serious one throughout the war.[44]

Many of the soldiers would "take to the brush when started to another part of the State." When Colonel Hobby's regiment was ordered to Galveston, so many of his men refused to obey that there was not a sufficient force to arrest them. However, this was not the first time that troops had refused to obey orders.[45] For instance, in October, 1863, several companies of the state troops refused to go into Louisiana, "even to scout."[46]

About thirty miles from Bonham, between two and four hundred disaffected men collected at three camps close enough together to concentrate within two hours. They picketed every road in that vicinity so perfectly that not a man, woman, or child could approach without their knowledge of it. About one thousand conscripts and deserters

---

[41] Rowland, *op. cit.*, V, 442-43.
[42] *O. R.*, ser. I, vol. XXVI, pt. II, p. 285.
[43] *Ibid.*, p. 236.
[44] *Ibid.*, vol. XLVIII, pt. II, pp. 1308-9, 1313, 1289, 544; vol. XXVI, pp. 352, 401, 398, 522, 330, 331, 344, 455, 456; and *passim*.
[45] *Ibid.*, vol. XXVI, pt. II, p. 522.   [46] *Ibid.*, p. 363.

from the army and militia were in the woods in that district.[47] In October, 1863, Henry Boren, one of the leaders of the disloyal, proposed to the Confederate military authorities that he and his band be sent to the frontier for service. In order to get them to return to duty, McCulloch consented, but he refused to allow them to select their officers.[48] On November 9, three hundred three deserters came out of the brush in a body and reported. Most of them were from the regiments of Colonels Terrell, Lane, Stevens, Alexander, Martin, Hubbard, and Hawpe. Besides those who came in a body, there were three hundred thirty-five others who reported at the enrolling office.[49] McCulloch had been instructed on November 6 to use all his troops, if necessary, to "make a clean sweep" of the camps of deserters, since it was necessary that they "be broken up at all hazards."[50]

But there were still some who refused to come in, and on November 28, 1863, General Webb ordered that the homes of the delinquent persons be searched. If the men could not be found, all arms, ammunition, meat, and other provisions were to be taken and the women were to be told that the taking of provisions would continue until the men came in.[51]

In the same year about two thousand deserters "fortified themselves near the Red River, and defied the Confederacy. At last account they had been established [there] . . . eight months, and [during this time] were constantly receiving accessions of discontented rebels and desperadoes."[52]

From the account given, it is clear that during 1863 the forcing of men into the army and the seizure of provisions under the tax-in-kind law produced great dissatisfaction

[47] *Ibid.*, pp. 329, 331, 330, 344.
[48] *Ibid.*, p. 352.
[49] *Ibid.*, p. 401.
[50] *Ibid.*, pp. 393-94, 398.
[51] *Ibid.*, pp. 455-56.
[52] *A. C.* (1863), p. 829.

among both soldiers and citizens. Moreover, the soldiers complained of their rations, and two serious riots occurred in Galveston. In one case, the men, after declaring they did not have sufficient to eat, "turned their guns on the town and compelled the commandant to give them what they wanted." In the other, the soldiers took their meagre rations into the street and burned them. Then they demanded better food and got it. Sometimes there were as many as fifty or sixty deserters a day.[53]

As the war continued and the struggle became more hopeless, conditions grew worse. By the spring of 1865, the demoralization of the army in Texas was very extensive. In all of the counties, from San Antonio and Austin up to the mountains, the soldiers were returning in large numbers. In some places they notified the enrolling officer and provost-marshal that their services were no longer needed. Benavides pledged not to fight the United States any longer, but when the time came, to go into Mexico and fight the Republic's enemies.[54] Many of the soldiers felt that the cause of the South was lost, and so, at the first approach of the enemy, they laid down their arms. General Magruder reported to General E. Kirby Smith that there was so much animosity toward certain classes of citizens that he must have protection for them against the deserters, who were far more dreaded than the northern army.[55] Four hundred soldiers at Galveston attempted to desert their post, taking their arms with them. The troops of that district could no longer be relied upon.[56] They considered the contest hopeless, and at least one half of the troops were ready to desert. They said, "We are whipped."[57]

[53] *Ibid.*
[54] *O. R.*, ser. I, vol. XLVIII, pt. II, p. 17; Aughey, *Tupelo*, pp. 341, 344.
[55] *O. R.*, ser. I, vol. XLVIII, pt. II, p. 1289.
[56] *Ibid.*, p. 1308.
[57] *Ibid.*, pp. 1313-14.

There is no doubt that many of the soldiers who deserted just before the close of the war deserted because they felt it was useless to continue the struggle and not because they wished the South to be defeated or because they had any love for the North.

CHAPTER IV

THE PEACE SOCIETY IN ALABAMA

THERE was much disaffection in Alabama and, as already noted, the Peace Society became very powerful in this state. Although many in North Alabama had opposed secession in 1861, the discontented caused no trouble during the first months of the Confederacy, since only the men who wished had marched away to war. But when the Confederate Congress began to discuss conscription, unionists and others who did not wish to fight for the Confederacy began to organize for self-protection and to cause trouble, just as they had in Arkansas. On January 19, 1862, Robert P. Blount, who was stationed in Greene County, informed Secretary Benjamin that in two counties the avowed unionists were organizing; three hundred men in one county had already encamped, and those in an adjoining county had elected officers to lead them. Though they had never stated any object for organizing, Blount believed that the two bodies meant to act in concert and free the prisoners at Tuscaloosa.[1] When the Federals came up the Tennessee River in February, they reported that many in Tennessee, Alabama, and Mississippi favored the Union and opposed the Confederacy, but that the people of Alabama and Mississippi were much more guarded than the Tennesseans in expressing their sentiment for the Union. The people in Alabama and Mississippi said, "We know there are many unionists among us, but a reign of terror makes us afraid of our shadows."[2] The unionists in all of these states asked for a small organized Federal force, with arms and ammunition for the unionists who could join the Federals and aid them in putting

---

[1] *O. R.*, ser. I, vol. VII, p. 840. Many unionists from Tennessee were imprisoned at Tuscaloosa at this time.

[2] *Ibid.*, pp. 155-56.

down the rebellion. Commander Phelps and other Federal officers advised that a Federal regiment be sent to serve as a nucleus for Union sentiment.[3] It is quite probable that many who flocked to the banks of the Tennessee River to see the Federal gunboats did so because of curiosity, and that some expressed their love for the Union in order to secure the protection of the Federals. Nevertheless, in April, 1862, it was reported that the northern counties of Alabama were "full of tories" and that a convention had been held in the "corner of Winston, Fayette, and Marion counties in which the people resolved to remain neutral"—an assertion which, many thought, meant they would join the enemy when it occupied the country. From these counties, men carrying the United States flag went across the line into Mississippi to stir up the unionists there. Bands of the enemy, which probably had been sent at the request of Phelps, numbered about three hundred men at Russellville, in Franklin County, Alabama; and other bands were roving over Franklin and Lawrence counties.[4]

The invasion of North Alabama by the Federals early in 1862 increased the discontent and disaffection. After the fall of Fort Donelson on February 16 and the retreat of Johnston to Corinth, the Tennessee valley was left open to the Federals. On April 11, 1862, General O. M. Mitchell entered Huntsville and his subordinates occupied other North Alabama towns. From that time until the close of the war the Federals marched to and fro across North Alabama, burning, robbing, destroying, and murdering. The suffering of the people was almost beyond imagination.[5] Mitchell's own report to Washington, in which he said that the lawless vagabonds and brigands connected with the Federal army were "committing the most terrible outrages—

[3] *Ibid.*, pp. 156, 421-22.
[4] *Ibid.*, vol. X, pt. II, p. 431; vol. LII, pt. II, pp. 299-300.
[5] *Ibid.*, vol. XXIII, pt. I, pp. 245-49; Fleming, *Civil War and Reconstruction in Alabama*, pp. 62, 74.

robberies, rapes, arson, and plundering," helps to substantiate the charges made against the army by the citizens.[6]

As a result of the suffering of the people, the protection afforded the unionists by the Yankee troops, and the disaffection caused by the conscription law, the disaffected element, which was made up of unionists, tories, and "mossbacks" or conscripts, began to cause much trouble to the loyal citizens and to the Confederacy.[7] It may have been at this time, or at least soon after, that the Peace Society was organized. At any rate, the disloyal, protected by the Federals, began to work against the Confederacy and to carry out the specific purposes of the society.

While General Mitchell remained in Huntsville, the unionists became very active. Judge George W. Lane, a prominent unionist who never lowered the Stars and Stripes during the entire war, and General Jeremiah Clemens, who by this time had deserted to the Federals,[8] gave General Mitchell the names of several prominent loyal Confederates and advised him to send them to a northern prison—advice which he followed. Clemens asked to be allowed to go to Washington as a representative of Alabama in order to learn in what way the war might be ended; but, upon the advice of Stanton, he remained in Huntsville and used his influence

[6] *O. R.*, ser. I, vol. X, pt. II, pp. 204, 290-92, 295, 293. In fact, the conduct of some of the United States troops was such that Mitchell protested and gave orders to have the plundering, robbing, and indiscriminate killing and destruction stopped. —*Ibid.*, pp. 294-95.

[7] The unionists were those who remained loyal to the North; the tories included the unionists and all others who rebelled against the authority of the Confederacy; the mossbacks or conscripts were those who hid in the woods to avoid the conscription officer.—Fleming, *op. cit.*, p. 113.

[8] *O. R.*, ser. I, vol. X, pt. II, p. 163; Fleming, *op. cit.*, pp. 125-26. Clemens was one of the coöperationists who led the opposition to the ordinance of secession in 1861 but voted for it. In April, 1861, Clemens declared that the acceptance of a United States judgeship by Lane was treason and that the north Alabama men would gladly hang him; but Mitchell informed Lincoln in May, 1862, that the appointment of Lane as military governor of Alabama would highly please north Alabama. Clemens in 1861 was placed in command of the militia of Alabama with the rank of major general, but in 1862 he deserted to the Federals.

for the Union. By May, 1862, the enemy had no trouble in buying cotton in Huntsville. This was facilitated by the unionists' openly acting as agents for the Federals.[9]

Still more disaffection was manifested when the conscription officers began their work. Most of the loyal men had already volunteered, and many of the disaffected refused to fight for the Confederacy. A few of the disloyal joined the enemy, but the majority of them hid in the woods and the mountains. Most of those who joined the Union army were poor men from the mountain counties of the northern part of the state.[10] During the summer, Governor Shorter reported that it was very difficult in several counties to enforce the conscription law.[11]

In October, 1862, C. C. Clay, Jr., reported from Huntsville that many of the people were openly defying the Confederate government, threatening loyal citizens, buying and selling cotton for the enemy, acting as spies and informers, declaring for the Union, and signing petitions for Union meetings. He believed some of the Confederate officers in Huntsville were disloyal. Many of the men were resorting to every expedient possible to keep out of the army. Some "were developing chronic diseases that their neighbors never suspected them of"; but many of the doctors detected these ailments without any difficulty and granted to the unfortunate invalids certificates which kept them out of the army. In fact, when the conscription act went into effect, health began to break down in all sections of the state. Many, overnight, became engaged in "manufactories or trades or mining."[12] Professor Fleming says: "There was never so

[9] *O. R.*, ser. I, vol. X, pt. II, pp. 167, 174-75, 638-39.

[10] During the entire war there were only about twenty-five hundred white men who enlisted in the Union Army, "not counting those who were enrolled in the spring of 1865."—Fleming, *op. cit.*, p. 88.

[11] *O. R.*, ser. IV, vol. I, p. 1149.

[12] *Ibid.*, vol. II, pp. 141, 142.—Fleming, *op. cit.*, p. 100. The above mentioned occupations secured exemption from the army.

much skilled labor in the South as now. Harness making, shoemaking, charcoal burning, carpentering—all these and numerous other occupations, supposed to be in support of the [Confederate] cause, secured exemption." And occasionally, when it seemed no reason could be found for being exempted, "an offending toe or finger was severed."[13] Still others went to the woods. Clay asked that a conscription officer be sent at once and suggested that a training camp in Huntsville would be a wholesome influence. He insisted that an example should be made of the leading traitors, to let the people know that the Confederate government had power to punish and to protect.[14]

By the close of 1862 the disaffected became more defiant. In Randolph County, the people defied the conscription act, and an armed force took the keys from the jailor and loosed the deserters. Colonel Hannon, who was sent to suppress the disloyal element and to capture the deserters, advised that the conscripts be sent immediately to Virginia, because it would be more difficult for them to get home.[15] It was useless to capture the "hill-billy" and "sand-mountain" conscripts, for "there were not enough soldiers in the state to keep them in their regiments. The Third Alabama Regiment of Reserves ran away almost in a body."[16]

By 1863 most of the substantial people that were loyal to the Confederacy had gone to war, and only "the old men, the exempts, the lame, the halt, and the blind, teacher, preacher . . . ," etc., were left at home. Most of them were convinced that the Yankees ought to have been whipped in

---

[13] Many secured a few hides, dug a pit in their back yard, and became tanners. The hides were carefully preserved and never finished because they would have to close the tanyard and go to war if no more could be secured.—Fleming, *op. cit.*, p. 101; Moore, *Conscription and Conflict in the Confederacy*, p. 54; O. R., ser. IV, vol. II, p. 141. For further unscrupulous methods by which exemptions were secured, see Moore, *op. cit.*, chap. IV.

[14] O. R., ser. IV, vol. II, p. 142.   [15] *Ibid.*, p. 258.

[16] Fleming, *op. cit.*, p. 102; O. R., ser. IV, vol. III, pp. 880-81.

ninety days, and that, since they were not, it must be the fault of Jefferson Davis and the Richmond administration. "Furthermore," says Professor Fleming, "the official class and the lawmakers . . . thought it their special duty to guard the liberties of the people against the encroachment of the military powers." They talked by the hour about the infringement upon the liberties and rights of the people by both state and Confederate governments.[17] Especially did the discussions over the hiring of substitutes, impressment, and tax-in-kind consume many hours. The "twenty-negro law" was considered a great injustice and many were convinced that it was "a rich man's war and a poor man's fight."[18] The short crops in 1862 had caused suffering which had increased the discontent. The lack of action against the disloyal and the conflict between the state and Confederate governments had done much to weaken both governments and to encourage the disaffected to defy them. Many of the people now believed that all that was necessary to end the war and to restore things to their former status was for the South to tell the North that it was ready to quit fighting; and when the South did not do this, the disaffected were angered and decided to do all they could to harm the Confederacy and its loyal citizens.[19]

Tories began to make raids on the defenseless population and to destroy railroads, telegraph lines, and bridges. When Colonel A. D. Streight was sent by the Federals in April, 1863, to raid North Alabama, cut the railroads from Chattanooga to Atlanta and to Knoxville, and destroy the Confederate stores at Rome, Georgia, he was guided on his raid through Morgan, Blount, St. Clair, Dekalb, and Cherokee counties by two companies of Union cavalry raised in

[17] Fleming, *op. cit.*, pp. 132-33.
[18] Schwab, *Confederate States of America*, pp. 195-96; Fleming, *op. cit.*, pp. 101-102, 134.
[19] *Ibid.*, p. 138; A. C. (1862), p. 9.

North Alabama.[20] Raiding parties sent out from the Federal gunboats on the Tennessee and the disloyal bands from the hill counties destroyed nearly all of the property in Lauderdale, Franklin, Morgan, Lawrence, Limestone, Madison, and Jackson counties.[21]

After the reverses of the Confederacy in 1863 the enthusiasm of the people for the Confederacy very perceptibly declined, because many believed the South could not win and dreaded the further sacrifices of war. As a result, not only the disloyal but many of the loyal began to urge peace.[22] Men refused to go into service, and desertions from the army increased. On July 28, 1863, General Pillow reported that he believed there were between 8,000 and 10,000 "deserters and tory conscripts in the mountains of [North] Alabama, many of whom have deserted the second, third, and (some of them) the fourth time." As fast as they were caught and sent back to the Army of the Tennessee, they promptly deserted and not only brought their arms with them but also stole from their comrades all of the ammunition that they could take away. Many of their bands were strong enough to drive away the small bodies of cavalry which were sent to arrest them. Several officers sent out to bring them in were killed. When too hard pressed by the Confederate forces sent after them, they ran "into the enemy's lines to elude capture." Pillow requested that when captured they be sent to the Army of Virginia, from which they would find it more difficult to return home.[23]

There was such a demand for peace and, as before noted, the Peace Society had become so strong that the leaders planned to elect, in the August elections of 1863, state and Confederate officers who favored ending the war on what-

---

[20] *O. R.*, ser. I, vol. XXIII, pt. I, pp. 245-49; Fleming, *op. cit.*, p. 67.
[21] *O. R.*, ser. I, vol. XXIII, pt. I, pp. 245-49; Fleming, *op. cit.*, p. 75.
[22] *Ibid.*, pp. 137-38.
[23] *O. R.*, ser. IV, vol. II, pp. 604, 680, 681; Fleming, *op. cit.*, p. 128.

ever terms could be secured. They succeeded to such an extent that the loyal authorities became suspicious, and investigations were made which finally led to the disclosure of the Peace Society. At this election "unknown" men were elected to the legislature and to other state offices, and six unionists, who favored ending the war at once and returning to the Union, were elected to the Confederate Congress. J. L. M. Curry, a staunch supporter of the Richmond administration, was defeated for the Confederate Congress because of his friendliness to Davis. Williamson R. W. Cobb, of Jackson County, one of the successful candidates for the Confederate Congress, was, after the election if not before, in constant communication with the enemy, and went into their lines several times. He was, however, expelled from the Congress by a unanimous vote. Yancey was replaced in the Confederate Senate by Robert Jemison, a former coöperationist and obstructionist in the secession convention.[24] W. T. Walthall, commandant of conscripts for Alabama, reported that the Talladega district had been carried by the Peace Society under circumstances that indicated treasonable influences. Men had been elected, he said, by "a secret sworn organization known to exist" and thought to have for its object "the encouragement of desertion, the protection of deserters from arrest, resistance to conscription, and perhaps other designs of a still more dangerous character." The leaders were believed to have been in communication with the enemy. While some of the members were "men of intelligence, influence, and prominent position," the election had been carried by the votes of deserters, stragglers, and paroled Vicksburg soldiers, who, Walthall thought, had been "contaminated by contact with Grant's soldiers." By this he evidently meant, says Professor Fleming, that they had be-

[24] *O. R.*, ser. IV, vol. II, p. 726; *A. C.* (1863), p. 7; Fleming, *op. cit.*, pp. 134, 138-39.

come members of the Peace Society.[25] Later disclosures concerning the Peace Society proved that Walthall was correct.

It will be recalled that this order maintained a line of communication between the enemy in North Alabama and Tennessee and the disloyal in Alabama as far south as Tallapoosa County. Some army officers and men connected with the conscription department were reported to be members of the society. Lieutenant J. Musgrove, conscript officer near Blountsville, Lieutenant Wilkerson of Blountsville, Clark Livingston and James Ooten, enrolling officers in Winston County, were members. Musgrove gave passes good for twelve months to deserters; and Lieutenant Wilkerson, commanding rendezvous at Blountsville, gave E. D. Meroney three passes at pleasure.[26] Major May was suspected of being a member, because, without orders, he withdrew all pickets from the Tennessee River, an action which left the Confederates without any way of watching the enemy. Pillow ordered his arrest.[27] Clanton was ordered to arrest all officers connected with the society and exterminate the organization in North Alabama. Many arrests were made, but the order was not crushed. Six months later (April, 1864), Colonel D. W. Jones, of the Ninth Texas Cavalry, who was sent against the tories in that section, found that the organization still existed among the tories, deserters, and other malcontents.[28]

[25] *O. R.*, ser. IV, vol. II, pp. 726-27; Fleming, *op. cit.*, pp. 138-40.
[26] *O. R.*, ser. I, vol. XXXII, pt. III, p. 682. E. D. Meroney was the man who escaped from prison in Knoxville, returned to his home in Blountsville, and to get information concerning the society, joined it. *See above,* p. oo.
[27] *O. R.*, ser. I, vol. XXXII, pt. III, p. 683. Among other men reported to be members of the "Peace Society" were: William Chamble, postmaster at Sapp's Cross-Roads in Walker County; K. Gambol and Wesley Prentice, from Blount County, both of whom had deserted from the Confederate army and were then acting as Federal spies. For names of other members see *O. R.*, ser. I, vol. XXXII, pt. III, p. 682.
[28] *Ibid.*, p. 683; Fleming, "The Peace Movement in Alabama," *loc. cit.*, p. 251.

As before noted, general disaffection and the organization known as the Peace Society were not confined to North Alabama. In the early part of January, 1863, soldiers had to be used to suppress "Unionism and treason" in Henry County, in the southeastern corner of the state.[29] About this time the Federals raided Coffee County. In order to clear out the deserters, tories, and runaway Negroes from Southeast Alabama and West Florida, Governor Shorter gave J. H. Clanton the authority to enroll men for the defense of that section. Believing it necessary for defense and hoping many who were hiding to evade the conscript law would come home and enlist to defend their homes and families, the Governor authorized Clanton to enroll conscripts in Coffee, Covington, Dale, Pike, Henry, and Barbour counties, as well as those not subject to the conscription law. Some of the conscripts came out of hiding and joined Clanton's brigade, but many refused and the disloyal continued to cause trouble.[30] In August Governor Shorter had to appeal to General Howell Cobb for aid in suppressing a band of deserters and conscripts who had for some time been infesting the lower part of Henry County, Alabama, and West Florida. They were in such numbers as to alarm the loyal citizens, against whom they were making threats of personal injury. A small force of state guards captured six or seven men liable for Confederate service and started them back under escort for safe-keeping; but a superior force in ambush attacked them, freed the prisoners, and killed one of the escorts. Cobb, who was already aware of the disaffection in that section, agreed that it was dangerous and asked for military authority to deal with the traitors. Since the men were generally not guilty of an overt act, it was useless to turn them over to a civil court, because they would be released.[31]

[29] O. R., ser. I, vol. LII, pt. II, p. 403.
[30] Ibid., vol. XV, pp. 939-40, 947-48.
[31] Ibid., vol. XXVIII, pt. II, pp. 272, 273-74.

In December, 1863, the Peace Society was discovered among the men of General Clanton's brigade, which was stationed at Pollard in Conecuh County. Just before Christmas between sixty and seventy of his soldiers mutinied and the whole scheme, which was to lay down their arms on Christmas day and go home, was exposed. Many of these men were from the poorer classes of Southeast Alabama and had suffered much during the war. They had never seen service and, being stationed near their homes, were under home influence. Some of them were exempts who had entered service because Clanton was a popular leader and they feared they might be forced into the army under someone else later. Others were substitutes and conscripts who had little patriotism and had been forced into the army or had responded to the Governor's call to come home to protect their families. Besides these, there were a few veteran soldiers. Being encouraged by people of their own section who were members of the Peace Society and having among their number some members of a secret organization—probably the Order of the Heroes of America—a number of the dissatisfied in Clanton's brigade had formed a peace society "with all the usual accompaniment of signs, passwords, grips, oaths, and obligations." They had bound themselves together "by solemn oaths never to fight the enemy, to desert, and to encourage desertion," and to do anything else that would aid in breaking down the Confederate government and ending the war.[32] Seventy of the men who were members of the society were immediately arrested and sent to Mobile for trial by court-martial. In January, 1864, Clanton had many more arrested. After he had made an effort to purge his regiment of those he thought would cause trouble, he, Governor Watts, and others begged for another chance for

---

[32] *Ibid.*, vol. XXVI, pt. II, pp. 548-49, 551-52, 556; Fleming, "The Peace Movement in Alabama," *loc. cit.*, pp. 249, 250; Fleming, *Civil War and Reconstruction in Alabama*, pp. 139-41.

the remainder of his regiment. Bolling Hall's battalion, which had been sent to the Western army because it had such a peace society in it, they said, had made a brilliant record at Chickamauga and in other battles. After the Battle of Chickamauga, its colors showed eighty-two bullet holes. Clanton believed his men would prove just as true to their colors if given a chance to fight. He insisted that the society had not originated among them but had been brought in by men from Hilliard's legion and Gracie's brigade and that but few of his men had joined it for treasonable purposes. Watts was anxious to have them sent to North Alabama, where they were bady needed.[33] Colonel Swanson, of the Fifty-ninth and Sixty-first Alabama Regiments (consolidated),[34] who investigated Clanton's men, said there seemed to be no leaders nor any general materialized plan on the part of the men; but that it seemed to be the general disposition on the part of substitutes, foreigners, and the poorer classes to accept terms and end the war. These people said that since they had nothing, there was nothing for them to fight for.[35]

Joseph E. Johnston was asked to take Clanton's brigade. Johnston was of the opinion that Clanton's army was too near home, and since they had been recruited from "a district and population not very loyal," he advised that the brigade be dispersed and sent to Polk in Mississippi. Johnston blamed Clanton for incompetency. Despite the pleas of Clanton and Watts, and despite the proof that the society had existed in the Army of the Tennessee long before this and the fact that the military court, trying the men sent from

[33] *O. R.*, ser. I, vol. XXVI, pt. II, pp. 552, 553, 554-55, 556; Fleming, *Civil War and Reconstruction in Alabama*, p. 141.

[34] The Sixty-first Alabama Regiment was composed chiefly of conscripts under veteran officers. It was evidently at first called the Fifty-ninth.—Fleming, "The Peace Movement in Alabama," *loc. cit.*, pp. 249-50; Fleming, *Civil War and Reconstruction in Alabama*, p. 140, n. 4.

[35] *Ibid.*, p. 140; *O. R.*, ser. I, vol. XXVI, pt. II, p. 550.

Clanton's command, completely exonerated Clanton, the men were sent to Polk and scattered among veteran troops.[36]

Dissatisfaction among the men in other commands also caused uneasiness. Major Cunningham of the Fifty-seventh Alabama Regiment reported just before Christmas that his men were aroused by the tax-in-kind law and the impressment system. Many of them, even some good men, were talking about laying down their arms if necessary, and going home to protect their families from what they considered the injustice of the Confederate government.[37] His regiment had been recruited in the counties of Pike, Coffee, Dale, Henry, Barbour, and Covington.[38]

In the spring of 1864, other attempts at making peace were in progress and the existence of a treasonable peace society in Middle Alabama was discovered. On March 1, Major E. Hollis and Captain W. C. Dowd, while sitting on the veranda of the Exchange Hotel in Montgomery, overheard a suspicious conversation between Colonel J. J. Seibels and a Colonel Holly. The names of Hon. James Johnston, a Dr. Tuggles of Columbus, and George Reese, of West Point, Georgia, were mentioned by Colonel Seibels in connection with a plan that he was forming or had formed. After Seibels left, Major Hollis demanded an explanation from Holly. The reply was that Seibels had decided— since the Lincoln government would listen to no proposition from the Richmond government for peace—that he would go to Washington to find out from Lincoln what terms could be secured for Alabama. Seibels further stated that the "Arkansas, or Sebastian, platform had taken in Arkansas and would take in Alabama." Holly disapproved of the plan

---

[36] *Ibid.*, pp. 548-49, 550, 553, 554, 555-56, 557; Fleming, "The Peace Movement in Alabama," *loc. cit.*, pp. 249-50; *O. R.*, ser. I, vol. XXXIX, pt. II, pp. 559-90.

[37] *Ibid.*, vol. XXVI, pt. II, p. 550; Fleming, "The Peace Movement in Alabama," *loc. cit.*, pp. 249-50.

[38] *O. R.*, ser. I, vol. XV, pp. 939-40; Fleming, *Civil War and Reconstruction in Alabama*, pp. 140-41.

because he believed it would prove very harmful.[39] How many favored Seibels' scheme is uncertain, but from developments in another section of the state, it is certain that the number was considerable.

As we have seen, it was about this time that the existence of a treasonable peace society in Middle Alabama was made known by Colonel Jefferson Falkner.[40] From him and others who made investigations, it was discovered that at least a majority, and perhaps two-thirds, of the people in Randolph County belonged to the society; that Lieutenant Colonel E. B. Smith, commandant of the reserves of Randolph County, R. S. Heflin, ex-state senator and then a lawyer of Randolph County, Dr. R. L. Robertson, a prominent Methodist minister, W. W. Dobson, a justice of the peace, David A. Perryman, late enrolling officer and justice of the peace, Captain William T. Smith, then at Demopolis commanding a company raised for conscript duty, and a large number of other citizens of Randolph County were members; that A. A. West and Henry W. Armstrong, two members of the legislature from Randolph County, were suspected of being members; that more than half of the men in Coosa and Tallapoosa counties, a large number in Calhoun and Talladega counties, and a considerable number in some other counties in Alabama, were members; that Colonel Hannon of the Army of the Tennessee and a large portion of his regiment were members of the order; and that the society extended into Georgia. L. E. Parsons, a "prominent, talented Yankee lawyer at Talladega," was a member and was thought to be the head of the organization. Lieutenant N. B. D. Armon, the district enrolling officer at Talladega, and the Board of Surgeons at Talladega on April 1, 1864, were

[39] *O. R.*, ser. IV, vol. III, p. 396; Fleming, "The Peace Movement in Alabama," *loc. cit.*, pp. 251-52.
[40] *See above*, p. 28.

also members. Major Hollis and Captain Dowd believed Colonel Seibels to be a member.[41]

The order did much harm. Members were sent to the armies to spread its doctrines. James Wood, who later was hanged by the Confederate cavalry,[42] and Thomas Lambert, who escaped to the enemy, told Falkner that Parton Vardenon had gone to Virginia to introduce the order into the Confederate army there and, if possible, to communicate it to the enemy; that J. W. Joiner had gone to the western army to get it through the lines; and that John H. Paster, Wood's son-in-law, was going to the Tennessee army to introduce it among the soldiers. They asked Falkner, who told them he was soon to join his command at Mobile, to introduce it to his men.[43] The society kept many men out of the army by having its members connected with the conscription department. As we have already noted, the Board of Surgeons at Talladega was composed of members. This board found many ailments among the conscripts who came to them for examination. A deserter, T. J. Pennington, who was a member, was arrested by A. R. Hill and sent to Lieutenant N. B. D. Armon, district enrolling officer at Talladega. Pennington gave the sign, Armon vouched for him, and the deserter was released and reached home as soon as his escorts. Soon after this he disappeared and it was said he had gone to the enemy. Members of the order claimed that the battle of Missionary Ridge was lost and that the surrender of Vicksburg was caused by the order.[44] Whether this is true or not, it is a fact that many soldiers deserted

---

[41] *O. R.*, ser. IV, vol. III, pp. 394, 396-98; Fleming, "The Peace Movement in Alabama," *loc. cit.*, pp. 252-55.

[42] The man who initiated Col. Jefferson Falkner into the Society. Wood and Lambert were lecturers or instructors for the society and they attempted to make Colonel Falkner an earnest worker in the society.

[43] *O. R.*, ser. IV, vol. III, pp. 395-96; Fleming, "The Peace Movement in Alabama," *loc. cit.*, p. 253.

[44] *O. R.*, ser. IV, vol. III, p. 398.

to the Federals before the battles of Missionary Ridge and Lookout Mountain. North Alabama regiments camped just opposite Carl Schurz's command. During the night many Confederate soldiers crawled over to the Federals. Schurz said sometimes when he arose in the morning, that the space between headquarters' tents was so filled with deserters that he could hardly walk. Most of them were from Alabama and were of the poor, ignorant class.[45] Many men also deserted just before the Chickamauga campaign and gave Thomas and other commanders definite information about Bragg's army, such as the number, amount of rations, location, and intended movements; and the Federals planned accordingly. During the battle the deserters continued to come in. Colonel Crose reported that about four o'clock [second day] "a deserter came in and informed us that Breckenridge's division of the rebel army was advancing towards the same point where we had been in such deadly strife during the fore part of the day, which statement was soon verified by the roar of artillery and small arms in that direction."[46]

By the fall of 1864, besides the conscripts and deserters from Alabama, there were many deserters from the commands in other states hiding in the mountains of North Alabama. After the fall of Atlanta the number of stragglers and deserters greatly increased, and it was estimated that six thousand of them were in the state—some in every county. Near the close of the year several thousand of Hood's army went over to the enemy and took the oath of allegiance to the United States or scattered to their homes. In many counties of Alabama, bordering on Florida, Georgia, and Mississippi, armed bands of deserters and tory citizens prevented the conscription officers from enforcing their orders. Loyal citi-

[45] Schurz, *Memoirs*, II, 69-71.
[46] *O. R.*, ser. I, vol. XXX, pt. III, pp. 582, 670, 671, 672, 673, 674, 529; Moore, *Rebellion Record*, XI, 74.

zens, especially in North and Southeast Alabama, suffered considerably from the disloyal.[47] Without question, some who deserted at this time were influenced by the Peace Society, although, no doubt, many men went home to protect their families from the outlaws and many others went because they felt it was useless to continue the war.

In the winter of 1864-65 General P. D. Roddy and several other Confederate officers were carrying on treasonable negotiations for peace with the Federal authorities. J. J. Giers, a brother-in-law of State Senator Patton, was in constant communication with Grant. In one of his reports to Grant, he said that Major McGaughey, Roddy's brother-in-law, had been sent by Roddy and another Confederate general to meet Giers near Moulton in Lawrence County to find out what terms could be obtained for Alabama. Major McGaughey told Giers that the people of Alabama considered that affairs were hopeless and wanted peace; and that if the terms were acceptable, steps would be taken to induce Governor Watts to accept them. In case the Governor refused the terms, a civil and military movement which would include three-fourths of the state would be begun to organize a state government. All of the leading men, McGaughey said, indorsed the plan, and all of the counties north of the cotton belt and those in the southeastern part of the state were ready to return to the Union. The peace leaders wanted the Washington administration to announce at once a policy of gradual emancipation in order to reassure those afraid of outright abolition of slavery; and to "disintegrate the rebel soldiery" of North Alabama, which, they said, had never been strongly devoted to the Confederacy. Giers also reported that Governor Watts was being approached on the subject. Andrew Johnson vouched for the good character of Giers and his loyalty to the Federal gov-

---

[47] *O. R.*, ser. IV, vol. III, pp. 880, 881, 1043-44; Fleming, *Civil War and Reconstruction in Alabama*, p. 129; Fleming, "The Peace Movement in Alabama," *loc. cit.*, p. 257.

ernment. A few days later Giers informed Grant that: "As various rumors have come into circulation in regard to the intended submission of several rebel generals, I was under the necessity of publishing an apparent contradiction of the report, as a premature knowledge of it among the Confederates might ruin their [the traitors] plans altogether. The object is to draw out all the Alabama troops with their leaders, for which the prospect now is very favorable."[48] To assure Grant that they were sincere, Giers told Grant he knew that Lieutenant W. Alexander, of Roddy's command, had sent without parole or exchange a number of prisoners from a Pennsylvania cavalry regiment into the Union lines. Several members of Gier's family who were at Valhermosa Springs, Alabama, had witnessed the act. Giers asked Grant to allow all deserters to remain south of the Ohio River in order to increase the number of Confederate deserters and further deplete the southern army. Many of the prisoners taken by Grant at Vicksburg were Alabamians. Numbers of them, after being exchanged, had gone within the Federal lines, and all had proved themselves loyal and reliable. At that time, Giers said, several hundred were "employed in various capacities on the lines of railroad toward Chattanooga, ... all of whom have proved themselves during the late rebel invasion in every way loyal and reliable."[49] In the spring of 1865, several subordinate Confederate commanders proposed a truce; and after Lee's surrender and Wilson's raid, it was a general practice.[50] No doubt many of these were loyal men who believed it was useless to sacrifice more lives.

Just how much strength the disloyal peace society in Alabama had and how much damage it did to the Confederate cause can hardly be estimated. But as we have seen, it car-

[48] *O. R.*, ser. I, vol. XLIX, pt. I, pp. 590, 592-93, 659, 718; Fleming, *Civil War and Reconstruction in Alabama*, pp. 146-47.
[49] *Ibid.*, p. 659.
[50] Fleming, "The Peace Movement in Alabama," *loc. cit.*, p. 258.

ried its activities into the army and was directly responsible for defection and desertion among the soldiers. It also kept deserters and conscripts from being sent to the army. In the early part of 1865, deserters and stragglers by the hundreds were scattered all over the state, and in half the counties of the state public sentiment was such that they could go and come without fear of arrest.[51] In the spring of 1865 the disloyal bands burned the courthouse in Coffee County, murdered some of the best citizens of Coffee and Dale counties, and made it dangerous for loyal Confederates to travel in that section. No session of the circuit court had been held in Dale and Coffee counties for two years, and Judge Cochran, the judge of the circuit, said he would not hold court in those counties unless protected by soldiers.[52] Much information was given to the Federals; and the disloyal, regardless of whether or not they were members of the Peace Society, did much to demoralize the soldiers as well as the people at home. Had the war continued until the fall elections, there seems to be no doubt that the disloyal peace organizations, together with the state rights peace group, could have and would have elected an administration which would have declared for immediate peace and refused to support the Confederate government any longer.

[51] *O. R.*, ser. IV, vol. III, p. 1065.   [52] *Ibid.*, pp. 1043-44.

CHAPTER V

DISAFFECTION IN GEORGIA, FLORIDA, AND MISSISSIPPI

Georgia

DISAFFECTION in Georgia was of considerable extent; as already noted, the Peace Society existed in West Georgia and was in communication with the peace organization in Alabama. Either this order or the Order of the Heroes of America, which had a large membership in North Carolina and Tennessee just across the Georgia line, or perhaps both organizations, existed also in North Georgia.

As has already been stated, there was much opposition to secession in this section of Georgia in 1861, and disaffection toward the Confederacy was manifested from the beginning. In Green, Sumter, Milton, Troup, Pickens, Fannin, Lumpkin, Newton, Rabun, Union, Gilmer, and practically all of the other mountain counties which had bitterly opposed separation in 1861, the Union sentiment remained strong and many refused to lower the Stars and Stripes after the ordinance of secession was passed. The Union sentiment in Jasper, Pickens County, was such that "a United States flag was raised upon a pole, soon after secession, and kept afloat in bold open defiance of Confederate authorities for several weeks." Many loyal Confederates appealed to Governor Brown to send soldiers to cut the pole down; but he, believing such an act would perceptibly increase the disaffection, refused to have the flag disturbed. In answer to the request he said, "By no means; let it float. It floated over our fathers, and we all love the flag now. We have only been compelled to lay it aside by the injustice that has been practiced under its folds. If the people of Pickens desire to hang it out, and keep it there, let them do it. I will send no troops to interfere with it."[1] Later the unionists lowered the flag of their own accord. Governor Brown frequently showed his tact on other occasions in dealing with the disaffected; and by his leniency toward them and his consideration for the soldiers from the disaffected counties, he won over many of the lukewarm and kept down trouble for a while. When troops were called for, the mountain counties were given preference in arms, equipment, and accoutrements, and practically every county raised at least a company. Fannin and Lumpkin each sent one and Newton, which had many ardent unionists, organized five companies and raised $10,000 for aiding these military corps. But despite Brown's tactful and lenient policy toward the unionists and toward those who were merely apathetic, trouble began very early in Rabun, Union, Gilmer, and adjoining counties and continued until the close of the war.[2]

During the second year of the war there were many things which tended to arouse and increase disaffection for the Confederacy. Especially were the tax-in-kind, impressment, and conscription laws considered grievous. Many of the poorer people had never been "conscious of paying [a tax],"[3] and when someone—frequently a stranger—appeared and took one-tenth of their farm products and perhaps a team, a wagon, and two or three head of cattle, the people resented it. But this might have been borne had the conscription officers not appeared and demanded that the men leave their homes and fight for the Confederacy, for which they had no love. Added to these grievances was the criticism of Davis and the Confederate government by Alexander H. Stephens, Governor Joseph E. Brown, Robert Toombs,

[1] *A. C.* (1860), p. 338; I. W. Avery, *The History of the State of Georgia, 1850 to 1881*, pp. 135-36, 187-88, 320.
[2] *Ibid.*, pp. 188, 189, 197, 257, 320.
[3] Stephenson, *The Day of the Confederacy*, p. 91.

and other prominent men who claimed that their personal liberties and the rights of Georgia were being violated.[4] Governor Brown gave much support to conscription evaders and made desertion from the army seem less odious by declaring that the conscription law was an injustice to the citizens of Georgia and that no more conscripts should be enrolled under the law of October, 1862, until the state legislature had passed on it. He further announced that the conscription acts infringed upon the liberty of the people, and that Georgians "having entered into the revolution free men," intended "to emerge from it free men,"[5] and he said that he considered it his duty to sound the alarm to the people.

These criticisms and threats made by Governor Brown and others soon began to bear fruit. Not only did the disloyal at home determine to keep out of the army but many of the volunteers in the army decided to come home. As early as November, 1862, the secretary of war reported that more than half the men who entered service from Northeast Georgia "were at home without leave." Most of these men were hiding in the mountains to avoid arrest. They were volunteers and not conscripts, because up to that time the conscription laws had never been enforced in this section of the state.[6]

By the beginning of 1863, Rabun, Union, Gilmer, and adjacent counties had become "the refuge of a band of deserters and Union sympathizers, who organized a rebellion on their own account against Confederate authority and the peace of the State." No doubt in fulfillment of their vows to the Peace Society or to the Order of the Heroes of Ameri-

[4] Eckenrode says, "Stephens had a witch doctor's nose for smelling out infractions of the Constitution"; he "caused the [Confederate] government more trouble than all the traitors combined"; and "the government would have been justified in imprisoning him, his activities were so mischievous."—*Jefferson Davis*, pp. 320-21.

[5] O. R. ser. IV, vol. II, pp. 13, 130-31. *See above*, pp. 15-16.

[6] A. C. (1862), pp. 16, 494.

ca, they banded together under leaders to prevent their own arrest and to release from the jails those who had been arrested. Many of the bands had arms and ammunition, and, as did those in Alabama, North Carolina, Tennessee, and other disaffected regions, they subsisted by plunder. They became such a menace to the state and the Confederacy that Governor Brown declared them outlaws and sent Major Galt and Major Wynn to break up their organization. These men captured "some 50 of the ring leaders, headed by a deserter named Jeff Anderson, returned some 200 men directly to their commands, and hustled out fully 2,000 absentees."[7]

In 1862 the crops had been short, and by 1863 the people, of North Georgia especially, suffered considerably from the scarcity of food. Although liberal arrangements were made throughout the state for the relief of the families of the soldiers and others, the dissatisfaction with the war increased. Deserters and stragglers continued to collect in Northeast Georgia, where the Union sentiment was strong and where it was difficult to apprehend them.[8] After the military defeats of July, 1863, in Georgia as elsewhere many believed the South could not win. The result of this attitude was an increase not only in the number of those at home who refused to go into the army, but also in the number of the disaffected within the army. Desertion became the order of the day. It was at this time that S. A. Hurlburt informed Lincoln of the existence of the Peace Society in West Georgia and averred that moral causes would have as much to do with the downfall of the Confederacy as physical causes. His conviction rested on the belief that the rank and file of the southern army had come to believe that they were not fighting their own battles but the battles of the politicians, officers, and planters; and on the fact that in Georgia, Alabama, and Mississippi arrests were being made of soldiers and civilians

[7] Avery, *op. cit.*, p. 257; *A. C.* (1862), p. 16; *O. R.*, ser. IV, vol. II, p. 360.
[8] *Ibid.* (1863), p. 447; *O. R.*, ser. IV, vol. II, p. 360.

on suspicion of membership in secret Union societies.⁹ It is true that at this time, as a result of the military losses in 1863, the feeling that it was a "rich man's war and a poor man's fight," the fear of loss of property, and the criticism of the state rights group, there was among many a clamorous desire for peace. Many were too timid to demand it openly but continued to favor it secretly.

In 1864 the outlook was gloomy; the hearts of many failed, and the disaffection increased. When Sherman came into the state, many were glad to submit to any terms to prevent the devastation of the country.¹⁰ The disloyal were greatly encouraged in their work because of the disaffection shown by Governor Brown and Vice-President Stephens. While Davis was with Hood's army at Atlanta and in other places in Georgia, trying to rally the people to the cause, Governor Brown and Vice-President Stephens, who had not been in Richmond for nearly two years, were doing what they could to break down the influence of the Davis administration. When Davis called on the Georgia militia to aid in expelling Sherman from the state, Governor Brown treated his call with contempt and demanded that the Georgians who were with Lee be returned to do the fighting. No man in the state openly showed more disaffection than the Governor.¹¹ The day Davis closed his campaign of encouragement, Stephens, in Augusta, told the people "that the resources of the South were exhausted and that peace ought to be made. He even talked of entering into a compact with the Northern Democracy to control the policy of the Union."¹² Peace meetings were held and many were clamoring for a convention of all the states in which the differences

⁹ *Ibid.*, ser. I. vol. XXIV, pt. III, p. 588.

¹⁰ H. V. Johnson, "Documents from the Autobiography of Herschel V. Johnson, 1856-1867," *American Historical Review*, XXX (Jan., 1925), 334.

¹¹ *A. C.* (1864), p. 405; W. E. Dodd, *Jefferson Davis*, p. 336; Stephenson, *op. cit.*, pp. 147-48.

¹²Dodd, *op. cit.*, pp. 336-37; Jones, *Diary*, II, 283.

between the North and South might be settled and the war ended.[13] Soldiers continued to show disaffection. A large number of the Georgia troops stationed at Dalton said openly they would lay down their arms and refuse to fight any longer if they were ordered to move from Dalton.[14]

When Sherman started on his march across the state, the demand for peace increased. While he was in Savannah, a secret meeting of the disloyal in Tatnall and Liberty counties was held, at which resolutions were adopted and forwarded to Sherman. The resolutions stated that the undersigned citizens of Liberty and Tatnall counties were either deserters from the so-called army of the Confederate States or men above the conscription age who would never aid in the rebellion; that they would band together under the leadership of some suitable person to protect themselves against the rebels; that the occupation of Georgia by the Federals met their approval and they would render any service asked by the Federals; that they had opposed secession and regarded its supporters as traitors. Death was to be the penalty for anyone revealing any of the proceedings of the meetings or any of the obligations of the members of their band. Sherman replied to these people that he would do all in his power to encourage and defend them in their course; that if they would remain at home quietly, and call back their sons and neighbors from the army, he would furnish them ammunition to protect themselves and their property; that if the rebels did them any harm, he would retaliate; and that their produce would be protected when sent to market. In order that the Federals might be able to distinguish these men from the loyal Confederates when they brought their produce to Savannah, Sherman advised them to form a league and adopt some common certificate.[15]

---

[13] Dodd, *op. cit.*, pp. 345, 346.
[14] O. R., ser. I, vol. XXXII, pt. I, p. 13.
[15] *Ibid.*, vol. XLIV, pp. 827, 828.

Disaffection increased in the state, and the disloyal continued to give aid to the Federals. Lieutenant John L. West, First Florida Infantry of the Confederate army, who left his regiment on February 15, 1864, at Dalton, Georgia, reported to the Federals that Jos. E. Johnston had between thirty thousand and thirty-five thousand men; that he did not "intend to give battle at Dalton, but [would] withdraw toward Atlanta if pressed by Grant"; that the men had no shoes; that their rations consisted of Florida beef, which they could not eat, and of corn; that "the spirit of the army was in favor of peace. The men re-enlist only to get furloughs and never return."[16] The demand for peace and the disaffection continued in Georgia until the war closed.

FLORIDA

In West Florida, across the line from Alabama and Georgia where the Peace Society existed,[17] there were regularly armed disloyal bands, and much disaffection also existed in other sections of the state.

In Florida "the term, 'Union man', ... was applied during the Civil War to those who were known to have consciously aided, abetted, or furthered in some fashion by word or deed the cause of the Union in its conflict with the Confederacy."[18] The "unionists" might be divided into two classes: first, the foreigners and men of northern birth who had recently come to Florida; second, the poor native southern whites who did not wish to fight for anyone. The first class was found chiefly in seaport towns and usually was possessed of property. Many of the foreigners were Germans who, with the northern whites, were against slavery; all of them were anxious to protect their property. The second class, the poor whites, were backwoodsmen who had to spend all of their time and energy in making a living and

[16] *Ibid.*, vol. XXXV, pt. II, p. 13. [17] *Ibid.*, pp. 12, 13.
[18] Davis, *The Civil War and Reconstruction in Florida*, p. 243.

who knew nothing about the issues of the war. The loss of a few head of stock, or the failure of a five-acre crop meant temporary ruin for them. They caused no trouble until the conscription officers appeared.[19]

Since the class of unionists composed of foreigners and men of northern birth were probably more interested in saving their property than in saving the Union, they remained quiet until their possessions were endangered. But from 1862, when the Federals entered Jacksonville, until the close of the war, this class of unionists, under the guidance and protection of the Federals, kept up a pretense both of being in the Union and of reconstructing Florida.[20] In the spring of 1862, the Federals occupied Jacksonville. After a meeting with Sherman, a mass meeting, at which about one hundred men were present, was held in the public square. Resolutions were passed declaring the ordinance of secession null and void because it had not been voted on by the people. A man formerly of New Jersey was the author of the resolution and a recent Vermonter presided at the meeting.[21] Upon the advice of Sherman, a second meeting was held, which provided for the election of state officers in April. During the stay of the Federals, the unionists loudly proclaimed their loyalty to the Federal government. When the city was ordered abandoned, they were horror-stricken and many fled. Practically all of these men were mainly interested in saving their property.[22] When the Federals left, the "political reorganization" collapsed. When the Yankees returned to Jacksonville in the spring of 1863, a second attempt at reconstruction was made by the same class of people and for the same reason. Again it collapsed, and many of the unionists fled when the Union army left. In the fall

---

[19] *Ibid.*, pp. 244, 246.
[20] *Ibid.*, pp. 255, 250-52; O. R., ser. I, vol. XXXV, pt. II, p. 301.
[21] Davis, *op. cit.*, p. 251; Moore, *Rebellion Record*, IV, 349, 325.
[22] Davis, *op. cit.*, pp. 252, 253.

of the same year the unionists in St. Augustine and in Fernandina, under the protection and guidance of the Federal troops, held political rallies; in May, 1864, a Union convention consisting of delegates from four or five eastern counties met in Jacksonville and again proclaimed their loyalty to the Union.[23]

When the conscription officers appeared, the poorer class of backwoodsmen began to cause much trouble.[24] Many of these men, not because of any love for the Union but either because they felt that their families could not live without their support or because they did not wish to fight, hid in the woods near their homes to evade service in the army. When the Federals came, these conscription evaders gave information concerning the Confederates.[25]

In the fall of 1862, Governor Milton appealed to the legislature to stop the speculation which was being carried on by traitors who were posing as loyal citizens. These men, he said, had partners in the North. They were not only charging the people of Florida extortionate prices for supplies and thus arousing dissatisfaction with the Confederacy, but they were giving information to the enemy, enticing slaves to leave their masters, and influencing some of the more ignorant people of the state to become disloyal.[26]

By the fall of 1863, the disaffection had greatly increased. Because of the conscription act, there were few men left at home. Those that were not in the army were hiding in the woods and swamps to evade the conscription officers. Because of the conscription law, which took the men away, the profiteering by unpatriotic people, and the poor crops, the families of 3,398 soldiers in the state needed help.[27] In

[23] *Ibid.*, pp. 253, 254; Moore, *Rebellion Record*, VI, 484. Names of some of the unionists are given on p. 485 of Moore, vol. VI.
[24] Davis, *op. cit.*, p. 259.
[25] *O. R.*, ser. I, vol. LIII, pp. 235-36; Davis, *op. cit.*, p. 258.
[26] *O. R.*, ser. IV, vol. II, pp. 57-58.
[27] *A. C.* (1863), p. 413.

the county of Taylor there were from eighty to one hundred soldiers' families suffering.[28] The order which required the sick to be brought to the camp of instruction for examination also increased the bitterness toward the conscription law. Governor Milton said there were many men in camp at that time who would never be fit for military service but who could be some comfort to the women and children, if at home. The disloyal were using the conscription law as a means of alienating the people.[29] In Washington County, forty men had been enrolled but only three could be brought to camp. Governor Milton believed that if they were allowed to volunteer, they would do so willingly.[30] "Two weeks ago they were informed they would be received as volunteers, and twenty of them marched fifty miles and volunteered, and the rest were preparing to come when it was ascertained that the offer to receive them was a telegraphic mistake, and the twenty escaped to their comrades."

In October, 1863, the deserters, not only from Florida but from the armies of Virginia and Tennessee, collected in such numbers in the swamps on the western coast of Florida that Governor Milton appealed to Davis for help to clear them out. They were in communication with the enemy; and in Taylor, Lafayette, and counties to the south they were in such numbers as to be a menace to the peace and safety of the neighborhood. The Governor advised that certain families who were in communication with the deserters should be removed to the interior beyond the Florida line. Many, if not a majority, of the citizens in West Florida, were said to be disloyal; at all events, they were advocating reconstruction and in Mariana had threatened to raise the United States flag.[31]

In the fall elections of 1863, most of the men elected

---

[28] *O. R.*, ser. IV, vol. II, pp. 839-40.
[29] *Ibid.*, p. 92.   [30] *Ibid.*, p. 93.
[31] *Ibid.*, ser. I, vol. XXVIII, pt. II, pp. 402, 403, 452.

to all of the inferior offices, such as justice of the peace and county commissioner, were men then serving in the Confederate army or alleged deserters from it. Governor Milton was much disturbed by this condition and informed Secretary Seddon that he would refuse to issue commissions to these men upon receipt of the returns of the election, unless the attorney-general said he must. The Governor said that these men were not needed in the state and he thought they should remain in the army. He further stated that there were deserters from other states in Florida, who were stirring up disloyalty and leading some to commit treason.[32] No doubt some of these were members of the Peace Society, the Heroes of America, or some other disloyal peace order whose business it was to create disaffection toward the Confederacy.

By 1864, conditions had grown worse in West Florida. Deserters from other states continued to join those in Florida, and they regularly organized themselves into armed bands for protection to themselves and for injury to the Confederacy. Colonel H. D. Capers, who was sent to Taylor County to break up the organization there, reported in March that he found it very difficult to deal with them. Instead of having regularly organized camps, they concealed themselves in the community near their homes. At the home of William Strickland, leader of one of the bands, Capers captured the muster-roll and the constitution of the organization known as the Independent Union Rangers, which gives an idea of the work of these bands. Their constitution read:

We, the undersigned, members of a company called the "Independent Union Rangers," of Taylor County, Fla., do agree that we will cheerfully obey all orders given by the officers we elect over us, that we will bear true allegiance to the United States of America;

[32] *Ibid.*, ser. IV, vol. II, pp. 879-80.

that we will not under pain of such penalty or punishment as a court-martial composed of ten men of the company, appointed by the captain, may inflict, give any information or speak in the presence of any one, even though it be our wives and families, of any expedition, raid, or attack that we may be about to undertake; that we agree to shoot or in some other way destroy any person or persons who are proven to be spies of the enemy, or any person who has carried information from our camps to any person through whom it may have gotten to the enemy; that all orders issued by our commanding officers relative to the killing of cattle and seizure of provisions will be cheerfully obeyed; that we agree to bring all property seized on our raids and expeditions to such place as our commanding officers may direct for the common benefit of all concerned, and in case of a division the captain shall make such distribution as to him seems most just; that we agree to make known any meetings or traitorous proceedings, or any violation of any orders of the superior officers, to our captain as soon as possible; that we agree to punish by death, or such other punishment as a court-martial may inflict, any person who may desert or entice others to do so, or shall treat with contempt his officer or weaken his authority in any way, or shall plunder or abuse any person known to be friendly to us.[33]

This paper was signed by thirty-five men who formed that company. In Strickland's home were also found "2,000 rounds of fixed ammunition for the Springfield musket, several barrels of flour from the U. S. Subsistence Department, and several other articles which evidenced the regularity of their communication with the enemy's gun-boats".[34]

These disloyal bands came from their homes in the swamp, raided the plantations near by, which produced large quantities of grain and bacon for the Confederates, and returned home. Having positive evidence of their disloyalty and being unable to capture them, Colonel Capers ordered the families of the disloyal to move, and then he

[33] *Ibid.*, ser. I, vol. LIII, pp. 317, 318-19.
[34] *Ibid.*, pp. 317, 319.

had the homes on both banks of the Econfina and Fenholloway rivers destroyed. After destroying the home of Strickland, he retired to a safe place to rest his men who, in getting through the swamp, had often been forced to wade through water three feet deep.[35]

After the burning of Strickland's house, Strickland sent a letter to Capers in which he proposed the terms upon which he and his band would leave the swamps. In his letter he said:

> I am anxious to hear from you, and you from me, for I cannot control my men since they saw you fire our house. . . . I ain't accountable for what they do now. As for myself, I will do anything that any half white man ever done, only to go into the Confederate war any more, though when I was in it I done my duty, I reckon. Ask Colonel Smith if I was not as good a soldier as long as he was captain, and would have been yet if Mr. Smith had of staid captain, but now I have went on the other side and tried what we call United States of Taylor, but I find it is like the Confederate men—more wind than work. As for myself, I ain't agoing in for any order, only to stay with Mr. Johnson and help him tend to his stock, and I will help him to pen or drive cattle for you, but my oath will not permit me to fight any more. If you will send and get me an exemption and my men that have taken the oath to stay in Taylor and raise stock for you they will do so, but they will not go into war if you had as many again men and dogs, for our title is Florida Royals, and if we can't get a furlough from Mr. Jeff. Davis during the war you will find our title right for a while; so I remain a flea until I get a furlough from headquarters, and when you put your thumb on me and then raise it up I will be gone. I give you my respects for the good attentions you paid to my wife, for it was not her notion for me to do as I was doing. Just set me and my men free from the war and we will try with leave to get corn till we make [it]. If not, you can go to moving the steers out of the adjoining three counties. So here is my love for the good atten-

[35] *Ibid.*, pp. 317, 318.

tions for my wife and child. If the war lasts long enough and you will raise him to be a soldier he will show the spunk of his daddy.

So I remain, W. W. Strickland,

Florida Royals.[36]

This letter shows that these people had no special love for the Union and would have caused no trouble to the Confederacy had they not been required to go to the army. The language of the letter convinces one that Strickland was not the author of the constitution of the Independent Union Rangers. Since he, perhaps, was above the average man in the swamps, it seems quite probable that the Federals or some disloyal person from another region prepared the compact entered into by these men.

The Confederate officers believed it better to temporize with these men than to send them back to the swamps; yet they knew that if they granted their request there were numerous other bands that would demand as much or more. The Confederate officers, therefore, decided that all deserters must be sent back to their commands but that the conscripts who had never been in the army could be employed to tend and drive beef provided they voluntarily gave themselves up to the Confederate officers. Strickland was asked to meet Colonel Capers under a flag of truce and arrange matters.[37]

Believing that the disloyal bands had induced many soldiers to desert, General W. M. Gardner, commander of the district on March 18, 1864, issued an order stating that all deserters belonging to such bands and not giving themselves up by a certain date should be shot wherever found, if they were armed; and that families of deserters and other disloyal men should be sent into the interior and their homes and property destroyed.[38]

[36] *Ibid.*, p. 319.
[37] *Ibid.*, p. 320.
[38] *Ibid.*, pp. 320-21.

In many other swamp sections, bands of deserters and conscripts collected and raided the plantations, enticed the slaves to leave, and in general menaced the Confederacy. They were in communication with the Federals, who furnished them food and arms.[39] In the spring of 1864 "10,000 blankets and 6,000 pairs of shoes intended to supply troops [in Florida] were captured" by the deserters. At another time the disloyal planned to capture the Governor, but he was warned of the plot and escaped.[40]

In Washington County there were many deserters—indeed, a large portion of the citizens were said to be disloyal. They were in constant communication with the enemy, which was at that time massing forces on Santa Rosa Island. The sheriff of the county and other influential citizens, Governor Milton reported, had gone to the enemy, taking their horses with them for the purpose of guiding the Yankees on raids. Just previous to this, the Union commander had reported that there were many deserters in the woods and that several regiments of cavalry could be raised by promising all who would enlist safe conduct within the Union lines.[41]

The disaffection was increased at this time by the impressment officers, to whom reference has been made, who were accused of taking all of the food and stock and leaving even the soldiers' families destitute. The failure of crops in some sections caused great suffering. The number of deserters in West Florida grew rapidly. Some joined the enemy. Governor Milton believed the impressment law was responsible for the growing disaffection. When fifty-two men from "the best drilled and most reliable company in West Florida . . . deserted with their arms, [and] some of whom joined the enemy," the Governor said they were "indignant at the heartless treatment of the rights of citizens." The Florida

---

[39] *Ibid.*, vol. XXXV, pt. II, pp. 4-5, 64, 215; ser. I, vol. XXVIII, pt. II, p. 273; ser. I, vol. LIII, pp. 309, 337, 319, 320.

[40] Davis, *op. cit.*, p. 261. [41] *O. R.*, ser. IV, vol. III, p. 16.

soldiers in Northwest Georgia and Virginia were much dissatisfied because of the taking of supplies, and Milton believed they would come home to protect and care for their families if the impressment agents were not more reasonable and just. Reports from Calhoun and Hernando counties stated that agents had taken even the milch cows from dependent soldiers' families, some of whom had not had a "grain of corn in the last three weeks, nor any likelihood of their getting any in the next three months."[42]

In August, 1864, Colonel Hatch of the Union army reported that "500 Union men, deserters, and negroes [were] ... raiding towards Gainsville".[43]

These organized bands continued to plunder throughout the war and, near the end of it, they became more numerous. It is difficult to estimate the number and influence of Union sympathizers in Florida during the war. Out of approximately seventy-five thousand white inhabitants in 1861 there were probably only four thousand who could be called Union sympathizers, but their influence in parts of Florida caused considerable trouble. By 1865, there were twice as many, but only about one thousand three hundred whites enrolled in the Union army.[44] The records show that about twenty-four hundred conscripts were enrolled in Florida.[45] Many of these were not out-and-out unionists, but because they did not wish to fight they became passive Union sympathizers. Over two hundred of those who deserted were returned to the army.[46]

MISSISSIPPI

Just when the Peace Society was organized in Mississippi is uncertain, but it seems quite probable it was started in 1862, about the time that the conscription act was passed and

[42] *Ibid.*, pp. 47, 45-46, 48.
[43] Davis, *op. cit.*, p. 260.
[44] *Ibid.*, pp. 245, 246; O. R., ser. III, vol. IV, p. 1269.
[45] *Ibid.*, ser. IV, vol. III, p. 1101.
[46] *Ibid.*, p. 1109.

the unionists and others who opposed entering the Confederate army organized to keep from being forced to do so.

During 1861 there was but little disaffection manifested toward the Confederacy. However, in Corinth there was one newspaper which openly opposed the Confederacy and favored the reconstruction of the old Union.[47] Professor Boynton, of the Department of Chemistry and Mineralogy in the University of Mississippi, was dismissed because of his Lincoln sympathies,[48] and there were many other staunch unionists in the state, especially in the northeastern counties.[49] By the opening of the second year of the war, disaffection had increased. When the conscription act was passed and the conscription officers began their work, the discontent assumed large proportions. When the exemption clauses became known, a great protest arose from all parts of the state, which gave much encouragement to the men who wished to remain at home. Many of the conscription officers were young, inefficient men, for whom the majority of the people had no respect. They made themselves odious by showing great partiality in granting exemptions. Senator James Phelan wrote President Davis:

> Never did a law meet with more universal odium than the exemption of slave owners . . . its injustice, gross injustice, is denounced even by men whose position enables them to take advantage of its privileges. Its influence upon the poor is most calamitous, and has awakened a spirit and elicited a discussion of which we may safely predicate the most unfortunate results. . . . It has aroused a spirit of rebellion . . . and bodies of men have banded together to resist; whilst in the army it is said it only needs some daring man to raise the standard to develop a revolt.[50]

[47] *Eastern Clarion* (Paulding, Miss.), April 19, 1861.
[48] *Ibid.*, Sept. 22, 1861.
[49] Rev. John H. Aughey, *Tupelo*, pp. 76, 78, 180, 333, 203, 266, 367, 383, and *passim*. See above, p. 46 n.
[50] O. R., ser. I, vol. XVII, pt. II, p. 790.

Phelan further stated that great bodies of men of conscription age, claiming to be paroled soldiers, were traveling all over the country, to their homes or otherwise; that all they had to do to go unmolested was to state that they were paroled.[51]

Senator Phelan was not mistaken when he reported that men were organizing to resist the conscription law. In Northeast Mississippi, even before the law went into effect, the unionists and others who did not wish to fight for the Confederacy began to organize and hold secret meetings "in order to devise the best methods for evading the law".[52] When the law went into effect, many of them "who would not muster nor be enrolled as conscripts resolved to escape to the Federal lines." Squads led by "skillful guides who could course it from point to point through the densest forests, with the unerring instinct of the panther or the catamount or aborigines, . . . reached the Union army, [and] enlisted."[53] The secret organizations "had countersigns so as to recognize friends and discern enemies. *Taisez vous* was the countersign known by the loyalists [loyal to the Union] from the Ohio river to the Gulf of Mexico. The recognition of it was *Oui, Oui* (pronounced we, we)." Aughey, the head of the organization in Tishomingo County, says this countersign was never discovered by the Confederates during the entire war.[54] Besides this countersign, others were used. In Tishomingo County "The Union Forever"[55] and also the words "Liberty and union, now and forever, one and inseparable" were used as passwords.[56] In case a member of the organization visited the home of a brother, a knock which was the preconcerted signal of recognition among the members of the unionist organization would admit

[51] *Ibid.*, p. 791.
[52] Aughey, *Tupelo*, p. 77.
[53] *Ibid.*, p. 78.
[54] *Ibid.*, p. 77.
[55] *Ibid.*, p. 80.
[56] *Ibid.*, p. 62.

him promptly even if it were at the midnight hour.[57] Both men and women belonged to the organization.[58]

Tishomingo, Tippah, Pontotoc, and Itawamba counties in northeastern Mississippi were filled with unionists. In Tishomingo County, which had given the Union delegates to the secession convention a majority of fourteen hundred, Union sentiment could be expressed with entire safety in many localities. One had to be careful in Corinth, Iuka, and Rienzi because of the Confederate training camps located in these places, which sent out cavalry to arrest and maltreat those suspected of disaffection to the Confederacy.[59]

By the summer of 1862 disloyalty was more pronounced, and both the loyal civilians and the Confederate cavalry were ferreting out, punishing, and persecuting disloyalists. Few of those even suspected of disloyalty to the Confederacy dared sleep at home because of the self-constituted vigilance committees. Most of the refugees sought out "some jungle or copse . . . [and] improvised a rude arbor or den in which they spent the night, and to which they betook themselves when an alarm was given by their families or friends."[59] Certain places high enough to serve as signal stations were named in each community, and a fire on each one was the signal for some specified message. In Tishomingo County, in one community the following names were given to the hills by the disloyal organization: Mount Sinai, Mount Nebo, Pisgah, Hermon, and Horeb. A call to an ordinary meeting of the unionists was a fire kindled on certain of these hills, while fires on certain others served as danger signals and calls to special meetings.[60]

About ten o'clock one night, in April, 1862, the Reverend Mr. Aughey discovered flames rising high from Horeb and Hermon, which indicated an urgent call. Concluding

[57] *Ibid.*, p. 61.
[58] *Ibid.*, pp. 79-80.
[59] *Ibid.*, p. 76.
[59a] *Ibid.*, p. 78.
[60] *Ibid.*, pp. 78-79.

from the nature of the signal that "either some impending danger was to be guarded against or some Unionist had been wounded or slain," he immediately notified five unionists "who were in hiding . . . awaiting the return of the guides who had gone with a squad to the Federal lines" and "they at once started to the place of rendezvous. . . .

"Quietly approaching from all points, human forms appeared, gliding noiselessly," until by midnight, when Mr. Aughey, the presiding officer, arrived, John Beck "reported ninety-four present, sixty-five men and twenty-nine ladies."[61]

Washington Gortney then rose to set forth the purpose of the meeting. He began his remarks by saying: "Mr. President—We are here assembled to determine what is the best method of evading the conscript law and keeping out of the rebel army. I favor enlisting in the Federal army." He further stated that he and James Reece had already joined the Federals, had fought at Shiloh, and were now members of the army at Farmington, which was assisting in the siege of Corinth.[62] He expressed the belief and the hope that Corinth would soon fall and that this would bring relief to the unionists of Northeast Mississippi.[63] After arguing that the unionists who remained at home in that section would be forced to fight for the Confederacy or be hanged or shot as many had been, he reported that three hundred men from Tishomingo County, and four hundred from Franklin, the county contiguous to this in North Alabama, were with the Federals at that time. After prophesying that Corinth would fall by July 4, 1862, and that not only Tishomingo County but probably all of the state would be taken by the Federals, he made a motion that a resolution

[62] Gortney and Reece had been allowed to pass through the Federal lines to converse with the unionists within the Confederate lines.
[63] Aughey, *Tupelo*, pp. 80-81.

be passed that it would be best for "the Union cause, to which we will ever adhere, for all of suitable military age to escape to the Federal army now besieging Corinth and to enlist in that army." Such a resolution was unanimously passed.[64] At this juncture a noise was heard and a squad of Confederates was discovered on the hillside near by. A messenger from the Confederates appeared to announce to the disloyal that he was a representative of a group of unionists. John Beck went over and found they had a former countersign used by the unionists. A skirmish ensued in which two unionists and four Confederates were killed.[65]

Soon after this the Reverend Mr. Aughey was ordered to attend a court-martial to be held June 1, 1862. After calling a meeting of the disloyal and finding that about one hundred others had received a summons to attend, he advised that they attend in a body and defend themselves if necessary. Before the day arrived, learning through one of their spies, Miss May Coe, that a body of Confederate cavalry from Corinth would be at the appointed place to aid the vigilance committee, they determined to try to escape to the Federal army stationed at Farmington.[66] When Aughey arrived at Rienzi on June 1, 1862, his heart was filled with joy to see General Gordon Granger's command carrying the Stars and Stripes as they followed the Confederates who were evacuating Corinth.

The home of David H. Aughey, a brother to "Parson" Aughey, was used as General Rosecrans' headquarters while the latter was in Corinth.[67] "Parson" Aughey became an agent for the disloyal, to sell cotton to the enemy[68] and carried information concerning the Confederate army to the Federals.

The disaffection was increased in 1862 because of exorbi-

[64] *Ibid.*, pp. 80-81.
[65] *Ibid.*, p. 83.
[66] *Ibid.*, pp. 86-87.
[67] *Ibid.*, pp. 87-88.
[68] *Ibid.*, pp. 91-92.

tant prices of food and other necessities. There was so much suffering that in March, 1862, the Mississippi legislature passed a law to create a fund, part of which was to be used for the support of the destitute families of volunteers in Mississippi.[69] By April some people in Natchez were advocating that the city be put under martial law in order to control the extortioners.[70] In fact, there was a continuous cry against them as time went on.[71] The *Eastern Clarion* said in May that "Unheard of prices . . . for provisions of almost every kind, to say nothing of other essentials, such as dry goods, clothing, etc., . . . are fast reducing a large class of our population to the condition of paupers."[72] Some believed the speculators and extortioners to be emissaries of Lincoln.[73]

The discontent was further augmented in Mississippi as in other states by the harsh criticism of Davis and the conduct of the war. "Newspaper Generals," who conducted innumerable parlor campaigns, were numerous. Politicians and others "sit in a comfortable chair and put up forts, plan campaigns, discipline armies, fight battles and win victories by the dozen per hour."[74] They showed Davis "to be a blockhead," pointed out the blunders of the ablest generals of the Confederacy, considered "every victory a defeat, and every repulse a last defeat." Some of the Confederate generals were too slow and some were too fast. "There was a constant complaint by the parlor generals from morning to night."[75]

When the Confederates began burning the cotton as they

[69] *Eastern Clarion*, March 28, 1862.
[70] *Natchez Daily Courier*, April 10, 1862.
[71] Various Mississippi newspapers from 1862 to 1865 contain many such protests.
[72] May 2, 1862.
[73] *Weekly Mississippian*, November 19, 1861.
[74] *Natchez Daily Courier*, June 4, 1862.
[75] *The Hinds County Gazette*, August 6, 1862, which quotes the *Natchez Courier* of June 4, 1862.

retreated from Corinth, in order to prevent its falling into the hands of the enemy, many families had to receive food from the Federals, and this turned their sympathies more and more to the Union cause.[76]

After the evacuation of Corinth by the Confederates, North Mississippi was open to the Federals, and those opposed to the war became more open in their criticism and in their efforts against the Confederacy.[77] As "the Union cavalry scoured the country in all directions," the unionists and other disaffected again felt safe.[78] "Parson" Aughey was not only given a pass through the Federal lines, but Rosecrans, to show his gratitude for Aughey's service, also sent Captain Gilbert, one of his staff officers, to conduct Aughey, his wife, and his daughter to the home of Aughey's father-in-law, who lived at Paden's Mills in Tishomingo County.[79] In June, 1862, General William Nelson, stationed at Iuka, asked Aughey to get information to him concerning the Confederate forces at Norman's Bridge over Bear Creek. To secure this, Aughey sent William and John Thompson, two unionists. One managed to get through the lines on the plea that he was going after medicine for his wife. He not only got three dollars worth of medicine but he also learned the number and position of the Confederates and the most vulnerable point of attack, which Aughey promptly reported to Nelson. Following the plan suggested by the spy, Thompson, Nelson's men made an attack the next night, and every Confederate soldier was killed or captured.[80]

By the middle of 1862, conditions were such in northern Mississippi that the loyal Confederates became alarmed and appealed to the Confederate War Department for aid, stating that there were many people in both Alabama and Mississippi who would certainly submit to the United States

[76] Aughey, *Tupelo*, p. 88.
[77] Chesnut, *Diary*, p. 179.
[78] Aughey, *Tupelo*, pp. 87-88.
[79] *Ibid.*, p. 89.
[80] *Ibid.*, pp. 92-93.

government if these states should be overrun by the enemy.[81] As stated in an earlier chapter, when Phelps and other Federals came up the Tennessee River in 1862, they reported that there was considerable Union sentiment in Mississippi; and they advised, as a result of the request made by the unionists, that a small Federal force be sent to that section to serve as a nucleus for them. The Yankees said that the disaffected Mississippians were afraid to come out openly and advocate the Union cause, but they believed that many would join a Federal force sent there. Captain Phillips, in his official report after the capture of Florence, Alabama, said: "We have met the most gratifying proofs of loyalty everywhere, across the Tennessee, and in North Mississippi and North Alabama, where we visited. . . . [The welcome given us] was genuine and heartfelt. . . . Tears flowed down the cheeks of the men as well as of the women."[82]

In the summer of 1862, the disaffection to the Confederacy became so pronounced in North Mississippi that Captain Pender was sent out to quell it. After he had ordered the shooting of ten tories—led by one Methuselah Knight—in the Poplar Springs neighborhood, Captain Pender, by a ruse of Paden Pickens and Paul Paden, two unionists serving as guides for the disloyal, was killed.[83] Many of the unionists, not only from North Mississippi but also from other parts of the Confederacy, were imprisoned at Tupelo.[84]

B. R. Johnson, the Confederate commander at Columbus, reported in April, 1862, that disloyal men from Alabama had appeared in that section and he was convinced they were there for the purpose of arousing the disloyal Mississippians.[85] It may have been at this time that the Peace Society, which was so strong in Alabama, was extended into

[81] *O. R.*, ser. I, vol. XVII, pt. II, p. 791.
[82] Aughey, *Tupelo*, p. 341.
[83] *Ibid.*, pp. 137, 134.
[84] *Ibid., passim.*
[85] *O. R.*, ser. I, vol. X, pt. II, p. 431.

Mississippi. A spy sent into the army in Mississippi at this time reported to General Pope that the Confederate troops were disorganized, mutinous, and starving; that the woods were full of deserters belonging to the northern counties of Mississippi; and that many soldiers still in the army threatened to throw down their arms and go home when they learned that the Federals were moving toward Decatur.[86]

During 1862, the disloyal in other sections were organizing to keep from having to enter the Confederate army. In the southeastern part of the state, especially in Jones, Jasper, Harrison, Jackson, and Hancock counties, there were many who refused to give any support to the Confederacy. Some of the soldiers who had volunteered from Jones County deserted and returned home after the "twenty-negro law" was passed. Jasper Collins, one of the returned deserters, said he did not propose to fight for the rich who were at home having a good time. In the latter part of 1862, he organized what was known as the Newton Knight Company. Newton Knight, from Jasper County, was captain and Collins was first lieutenant. In the beginning there were about sixty in the company, several of whom were deserters. Later the number increased to one hundred sixty-five, some of whom were from other counties, and even from other states. This band had its headquarters near Sosa, on an island in Leaf River. After making raids on loyal Confederates, the band would return to the island. One time they were successful in capturing a Confederate wagon train, but most of the damage done by them was to the loyal Confederates of Jasper and Jones counties.[87]

These local opponents of the Confederacy had no more interest in slavery than did many of the soldiers who fought loyally for the southern cause. Both groups believed that

[86] *Ibid.*, vol. XVII, pt. II, p. 5.
[87] Goode Montgomery, "Alleged Secession of Jones County," *Publications of the Mississippi Historical Society*, VIII (1904), 14-15.

they were fighting in defense of their homes and their rights.[88] Knight was in communication with the Federal officers at both Memphis and Vicksburg, and Collins was detailed by Knight to carry on communication between the Federals and the local unionists.[89]

It is alleged that Jones County seceded from the Confederacy and established the "Jones County Confederacy," with Nathan Knight as president, and that the population of this new Confederacy was increased from 3,323 to more than 20,000 by refugees from the Davis government.[90] Others say the county did not secede, that the county government was never interrupted, but that it went from the Union to the Confederacy during the war and back to the Union during the Reconstruction period without change of officers.[91] Although the secession seems to be a myth, it is true that, because of the notoriety resulting from the disloyal making the county their rendezvous and also because of the demonstrations against J. D. Powell,[92] who voted for secession, the loyal Confederates upon returning home petitioned the state legislature in 1865 to change the name of the county to Davis in honor of Jefferson Davis, and the county seat from Ellisville to Leesburg in honor of Robert E. Lee. This petition was granted, but during the Reconstruction period the former names were restored.[93]

Montgomery says that the bands, instead of numbering ten thousand as stated by Galloway, were never over one

---

[88] Thos. H. Woods, "A Sketch of the Mississippi Secession Convention of 1861, Its Membership and Work," *Publications of the Mississippi Historical Society*, VI (1902), 93-94.

[89] *Ibid.*, p. 15.

[90] G. Norton Galloway, posing as historian of the Sixth Army Corps writing in October, 1886, made this statement. See *American Historical Magazine*, XVI, 387-88.

[91] Montgomery, "Alleged Secession of Jones County," *loc. cit.*, p. 15; Alexander Bondurant, "Did Jones County Secede?", *Publications of the Mississippi Historical Society*, I (1898), 104-6.

[92] Powell was elected as an anti-secessionist but voted in the state convention for secession. As a result, he was hanged in effigy.

[93] Montgomery, "Alleged Secession of Jones County, *loc. cit.*, p. 16.

hundred twenty-five and usually numbered around eighty. Although evidence seems to show that Montgomery was more nearly correct in his estimate than Galloway, there is no doubt that "Newt" Knight's band and other disloyal people in this section gave the Confederate authorities much trouble, because these disloyal bands knew every path, and the character of the country made it difficult to apprehend them.[94]

During 1862 the exorbitant prices and the scarcity of the necessities of life, the ravages of the Federals, the Confederate military losses, the "Newspaper Generals," the vigorous work of the conscription department, and the work of the disloyal organizations had increased the disaffection and the desire for peace in Mississippi and elsewhere in the Confederacy.[95] Desertion had become such a problem that by December, 1862, there was an urgent demand for coöperation with the Confederate authorities to remedy the evil. Some urged that the state pass a law depriving a "deserter for all time of the privilege of elective franchise," inflicting "a severe penalty upon those who harbor him, or fail to give information of his crime," and declaring those evading the conscription act and those absent from the army without leave equally guilty with the deserter.[96]

Under Joseph E. Johnston's orders, General Pillow began to round up deserters and stragglers from the Confederate army. In February, 1863, General Pillow reported that he had ordered twelve thousand of this class to the Army of the Tennessee. Some of them, however, were from Tennessee and Alabama. No doubt he would soon have cleared out those in Mississippi and other states in his District who were avoiding service in the army had the War

[94] *Ibid.*, p. 18.
[95] *A. C.* (1863), pp. 651, 66; Kate Cumming, *Journal of Hospital Life in the Confederate Army of Tennessee*, p. 68; *Natchez Daily Courier*, March 11, 1863.
[96] *Natchez Daily Courier*, December 6, 1862, which quotes from *The Mississippian* (no date given).

Department not disapproved of his "steam roller" method of getting conscripts and stopped it.[97] In June, General Pemberton was informed that the southeastern section of the state "swarms with deserters from almost every organization formed in the sea-coast counties, and there are not less than 1,000 of them in the three counties of Harrison, Hancock, and Jackson," and that it would require "a good force of well-disciplined cavalry to get them back to the army."[98] Immediately after the fall of Vicksburg the *Richmond Examiner* announced that "'large numbers' were deserting Johnston's army at Jackson and going into the Union lines." The *Mobile Advertiser* said that these men were "whining for peace and reconstruction."[99] In August, a conscription officer estimated the number of stragglers and deserters in the state at five thousand.[100] General Pillow, on September 1, estimated that there were five hundred in the vicinity of Pearl River.[101]

The attitude of many of the influential citizens and their attempt at reconstruction must have given considerable encouragement to the disloyal who, in general, were of the poorer classes. On July 21, 1863, representatives from several towns met in Jackson, discussed plans for peace on the basis of a return to the Union, and decided to attempt to reorganize the government in conformity with the Constitution and laws of the Union. Sherman favored and encouraged their plan.[102] Judges Sharkey, Yerger, Poindexter, and other prominent men, most of whom were old-line Whigs and had opposed secession in 1861, headed the movement for peace.[103] At this time Judge Sharkey, ex-

---

[97] O. R., ser. IV, vol. II, pp. 403-4.
[98] Report from Harrison of Captain and assistant Adjutant-General of the Sea-Coast Section to General Pemberton.—*Ibid.*, ser. I, vol. LII, pt. II, p. 493.
[99] James W. Garner, *Reconstruction in Mississippi*, p. 53.
[100] O. R., ser. IV, vol. II, p. 717.   [101] *Ibid.*, p. 782.
[102] *Ibid.*, ser. I, vol. XXIV, pt. II, pp. 530-31; Garner, *op. cit.*, p. 52.
[103] *Ibid.*, p. 51.

Governor Brown, and many people in Vicksburg, Natchez, and other places in West Mississippi took the oath of allegiance to the United States. Many of the wealthy planters favored this peace movement.[104] *The Richmond Enquirer* said that they "had their 'patriotism corrupted by love of cotton' ";[105] while the *New York Times* said that nine-tenths of the inhabitants were anxious for peace and restoration to the Union,"[106] but this is hardly probable. No doubt many who up to this time had been loyal favored peace because they felt that the southern cause was lost and that it was useless to continue the bloodshed and suffering. Naturally the disloyal favored peace, but since it was still unsafe in many communities, and at least unpleasant in others, to advocate submission to the Federal government, many continued to work secretly for peace. Governor Thompson, in his message to the legislature in November, 1863, attempted to offset the peace movements by declaring that "independence, or that which was worse than death, were the only alternatives presented to the people, and the sooner the truth was fully realized and acted upon the better it would be for themselves and their children."[107]

Colonel Benjamin H. Grierson of the Sixth Illinois Cavalry, after he had made his famous raid in April, 1863, from La Grange, Tennessee, through Mississippi to Baton Rouge, reported that there were thousands of unionists who were ready and anxious to aid the Union in every possible way; and that had he been able to arm them, he could have added to his forces a thousand who were fugitives from their homes, hiding in forests and swamps, where they were being hunted by conscription officers with bloodhounds.[108]

By 1864, conditions in Mississippi had become even more

[104] *Ibid.*, pp. 52-53.
[105] August, 1863, quoted from Garner, *op. cit.*, p. 53.
[106] August 2, 1863, quoted from Garner, *op. cit.*, p. 53.
[107] Garner, *op. cit.*, pp. 52, 53.   [108] Aughey, *Tupelo*, p. 333.

alarming to the Confederacy. The suffering of the people who had fled from their homes when the Federals occupied Vicksburg and other places in the state was almost beyond description; and, as a result, many wanted peace at any price.[109] By the spring of 1864, public sentiment in the state was "much depressed." The secretary of war was informed that many of the men in southern Alabama and Mississippi who ought to be in the army were now even threatening to resist the Confederate authority.[110] It will be recalled that it was at this time that the Peace Society was causing so much trouble across the line in Alabama. Complaint was made in Mississippi that much of the trouble was caused by the failure of General Polk to inspire confidence and arouse enthusiasm among the civilians and troops, and Secretary Seddon was asked to send General Beauregard to that section.[111] Polk blamed the Bureau of Conscription for not arresting absentees from the army. He said that in his territorial limits there were ten thousand men liable to service who were evading it. No doubt many were holding some petty office or were engaged in some occupation which exempted them from military service. Polk also reported that a large number of disaffected people in Jones County had banded together and had raided the stores at Paulding in Jasper County; and that Captain Rison and a portion of his command had deserted their post and were plundering the country northwest of the Tallahatchee. Rison and his band plundered the loyal as well as the disloyal when they had anything Rison wanted. In compliance, perhaps, with his obligations to the Peace Society, Rison sent many messages to his friends in the army, in-

---

[109] *A. C.* (1864), p. 550; Josie Frazee Cappleman, "Local Incidents of the War between the States," *Publications of the Mississippi Historical Society*, IV (1901), 80-81, 84.

[110] *O. R.*, ser. I, vol. LII, pt. II, p. 635.

[111] *Ibid.*, p. 636.

viting them to join him. As inducement, he offered free quarters and brigandage.[112]

By the fall of 1864 conditions were such that Secretary Seddon appealed to General Richard Taylor, commandant at Meridian, Mississippi, to make some attempt to remedy the evils in that state. Seddon said that the deserters seemed to have no difficulty in any section of the country in obtaining shelter and protection, and that his reports showed that deserters and absentees from the army without leave abounded in Mississippi. The conduct of many men posing as Confederate officers increased the disaffection. They formed cavalry bands, without orders, and impressed horses for these bands. Men without special orders were going through the state, gathering up property and refusing to pay for it, and in most cases rendering no account of their acts or authority for their acts to anyone. Seddon appealed to Taylor to see that this was stopped.[113] In November, Governor Clark sent two companies of militia into Choctaw County to deal with the deserters. About five hundred were there and at least half of them were armed and in organized bands.[114]

Shortly before this, in October, Senator Phelan reported to Davis that the state "literally swarms with deserters," and that there seemed to be only a "Spartan Band" who were loyal to the Confederacy, "whilst the timid, the traitor, and the time-server are 'legion.'"[115] At the fall elections, he said, bands of deserters had appeared at the polls in some of the counties and defied arrest. Even good soldiers who were sent after the fugitives sometimes were persuaded to remain with the worthless bands. Phelan thought that ignorance of the consequences involved in the struggle, the seeming hopelessness of success, the fear of punishment, and the lack of money to aid the deserters in getting back to their

---

[112] Polk's report to the Secretary of War.—*Ibid.*, ser. IV, vol. III, pp. 445-46.
[113] *Ibid.*, pp. 688-90.
[114] *Ibid.*, ser. I, vol. LII, pt. II, p. 792.   [115] *Ibid.*, ser. IV, vol. III, pp. 707, 710.

commands, prevented many of them from returning to the army. To induce them to return, he proposed that Davis appoint loyal men in each state to address the absentees from the army. In order to get them to attend such a meeting, they were to be given the assurance that no one should be arrested while there. Anyone who agreed to return to the army should be given a special pardon for all past offenses in the army, and also transportation to his command.[116] Phelan's plan was not tried, but very likely few would have attended such meetings.

At the close of 1864, the inspector general said that the conscript departments in Mississippi, Georgia, and Alabama were "almost worthless"; that more men would be added to the army by sending the men employed in that department into the field than probably would be added by the conscripts they sent. At Brookhaven, Mississippi, 1,125 men were examined between April and October, 1864, and 807 of them were discharged as unfit for military service. During the last five months of 1864 only 235 conscripts had been started to the field from Mississippi; and if the deserters from that number were in proportion to those from the offices and camps of instruction, there was not a company of them in the army. There had been 537 conscripts enrolled during that time but 302 of them had deserted before they were started from the state.[117] Many men were exempted by the state; and, no doubt, many of the men on the examining boards and many of the conscription officers were members of the Peace Society. H. W. Walter, inspector general, said that every post was full of skulkers under details; that the "Quartermaster, Commissary, Ordnance, Medical, and Post Departments are full even to repletion"; that most of these men were young and healthy but when he approached a detail, "he thrusts into my face a certificate of disability.

[116] *O. R.*, ser. IV, vol. III, pp. 707-10. [117] *Ibid.*, p. 976.

The disease is occult, the name scarcely known to me."[118] At the close of 1864, the number of deserters in the state was estimated at seven thousand.[119]

The deplorable conditions of the country increased the demand for peace. Bands of deserters and stragglers roamed about, irregular bands of cavalry took horses, and the Federals took food and clothes. Men refused to go into the army, and many demanded that peace be made in time for the soldiers to make crops. In the northwestern part of Mississippi there were "large numbers of deserters" who robbed "friend and foe indiscriminately." Inspector General Walter said that William Crump, Sr., and James House, of Marshall County, were sending "with success their trains of cotton to the foe" and importing "in return luxuries not essential to the public welfare," and that Crump brought back "barrels of whiskey to brutalize the soldier already demoralized by straggling from the army or desertion of his country's cause." He was sure, he said, "that not less than 1,000 deserters . . . could have been found between the picket-lines in this section" during the last part of January, 1864. Prominent citizens of Holly Springs reported that "conscripts and deserters are daily seen on the streets of the town"; . . . that "Charles Smith, a private of the Thirty-fourth Mississippi Regiment, a brother-in-law of Lieutenant John's clerk, notoriously a deserter, has been repeatedly in the conscript office without molestation"; and that not one man had been sent to the army for several months.[120] In Tishomingo County—where, as before noted, the disloyal were organized—the United States military authorities granted permission to the people to hold regular sessions of the circuit, probate, and police courts on condition that they would do nothing at any session to injure the United States, and granted also the right to run trains on both railroads

[118] *Ibid.*, p. 977.
[119] *Ibid.*, p. 976.
[120] *Ibid.*, ser. I, vol. XLIX, pt. I, p. 950.

for the use of private citizens. In the early part of March, 1863, meetings were held in Newton and Kemper counties, in which resolutions were adopted expressing a readiness to submit to the authority of the United States and asking for the protection of Federal authorities against deserters, jayhawkers, and robbers.[121] Disaffection continued to increase steadily, and, had the war not closed when it did, the formidable peace party might have become sufficiently strong to have produced in the fall elections of 1865, as Phelan feared, a contest which would "tax the powers and pain the souls of the 'good men and true.' "[122] On December 29, 1864, one of the conscription officials said, "I believe there are this day in Mississippi alone a sufficient number of deserters, skulkers, idle officers, improper details, and useless exempts to give victory to any army to which they are sent."[123] Of course these men all favored peace, though many of them may not have belonged to a well organized Peace Society, and may not even have desired the Confederacy to fail.

[121] *Ibid.*, p. 612; Garner, *op. cit.*, p. 55.
[122] *O. R.*, ser. IV, vol. III, p. 710.   [123] *Ibid.*, p. 978.

CHAPTER VI
THE HEROES OF AMERICA AND DISAFFECTION IN THE CAROLINAS

NORTH CAROLINA

DURING the war there was much disaffection in North Carolina. The Order of the Heroes of America became widespread there and was in constant communication with the North.[1] Because of a red string worn in the lapel of the coat, in allusion to the Bible story of Rahab, the order was commonly known as the "Red Strings" or the "Red String Band." Although the Order of the Heroes of America may not have been organized until some time after the war began, disaffection and active opposition appeared in North Carolina the first year of the war and increased alarmingly as the struggle continued. As early as September, 1861, Rush C. Hawkins, commander of the Federal troops at Fort Clark, Hatteras Inlet, reported that "one-third of the State of North Carolina would be back in the Union within two weeks" if the United States forces were near enough to protect the people.[2] This was no doubt an exaggeration, though the loyalty to the Union, manifested when Hatteras was captured, is proof that not all of the people could be depended upon to support the Confederacy.

Disaffection was far from being confined to any one section of the state, but its first manifestation was in the East. As soon as the Federals captured the forts on the eastern coast, the citizens of Hatteras petitioned the Union commander at Hatteras Inlet not to treat them as rebels,

[1] *O. R.*, ser. IV, vol. III, *passim*; Hamilton, *Reconstruction in North Carolina*, pp. 63-64.
[2] *O. R.*, ser. I, vol. IV, pp. 606, 608.

since they had neither taken up arms against the Union nor voted to withdraw from it.³ Within a week, more than two hundred and fifty had taken the oath of allegiance to the United States and had promised to keep the Federals informed of the movements of the Confederates, in return for protection by the Federal army. Secret meetings of the disloyal were held in the counties bordering Pamlico Sound, and many acted as spies for the enemy. Hyde, Washington, Tyrrell, and Beaufort counties showed so much disaffection that the loyal Confederate citizens became alarmed. Many of the loyal men had volunteered, while all of the unionists and those that were lukewarm remained at home. Moreover, many felt that since they were already in the hands of the Federals, submission was their only course.⁴

Among the leaders who attempted to coöperate with the Federals were Charles H. Foster, who on account of disloyalty had recently been expelled from Murfreesborough in a meeting of loyal citizens of the town, and Marble Nash Taylor, a Methodist minister, who was accused of having given to the Federals information which had contributed to the ease of their victory. These two men went to New York, and in a meeting presided over by George Bancroft, the historian, helped to form a plan for the setting up of a new state government in North Carolina.⁵

On November 18, in accordance with the plan formulated in New York, a convention assembled, declared the ordinance of secession null and void, and ordered an election to be held to elect members to the United States Congress. Although there were only six or eight citizens at the convention, Foster claimed that forty-five counties were represented, either by delegates or by proxies.⁶

³ *Ibid.*, ser. I, vol. IV, pp. 611, 657, 658, 671.
⁴ *Ibid.*, pp. 606-9, 671; Hamilton, *Reconstruction in North Carolina*, pp. 81-82.
⁵ *Ibid.*, pp. 84-85.
⁶ Three elections were held to elect a representative to Washington and each time Foster was chosen but he was never recognized by the U. S. Congress.—*Ibid.*, pp. 86-87.

In Middletown, on the coast, secret meetings were held, and it was resolved to allow the Federal forces to land without interference, if they would guarantee protection from the Confederate vigilance committees.[7]

In western North Carolina disaffection was also showing itself. By November, 1861, Governor Clark wrote Secretary Benjamin that he was receiving "numerous communications from the North Carolina counties bordering on East Tennessee" requesting help against traitors.[8] Although the western part of the state had practically no interest in slavery, in the beginning it showed its loyalty by furnishing an undue portion of volunteers.[9] This weakened the mountain counties to such an extent that they were unable to protect themselves from the disloyal who were left at home, from the East Tennesseans, who began making raids, and from the vicious outlaw bands that collected in the mountains to rob and steal.

Governor Clark, of North Carolina, asked Secretary of War Benjamin for a force to protect these loyal people and to prevent the Tennessee traitors from overrunning the border counties and spreading disloyalty among the western North Carolinians. Two days later, the Governor informed Secretary Benjamin that Tennesseans had already visited the border counties and that some North Carolinians were showing themselves to be disloyal. Again he urged that a force be sent to put down the treason and to prevent its spread to adjacent counties. Conditions became so alarming in the mountain counties along the border that a recently formed regiment of loyal men in Buncombe County and a similar

[7] O. R., ser. I, vol. IV, p. 618.
[8] Ibid., vol. LII, pt. II, p. 209.
[9] "From Ashe to the Georgia line the thirteen mountain counties, with 68,000 population, had furnished by the last of October, 4,400 soldiers, one in fifteen, while the remaining counties furnished only one in nineteen."—Ashe, *History of North Carolina*, II, 660-61.

regiment in Ashe asked that they be sent home "to stay the fury of Tennessee treason."[10]

As before noted, it was shortly after this, on December 7, that Brigadier General W. H. Carroll informed General A. S. Johnston that a plan was on foot "for a thorough organization of the disloyalists in East Tennessee and the bordering counties of North Carolina."[11] Whether or not the Order of the Heroes of America was organized at this time is not known; but Governor Clark three weeks before this had reported the existence in East Tennessee of a treasonable movement of "formidable proportions," through the influence of which the border counties of North Carolina were "greatly excited . . . and a few . . . disaffected." By November, 1864, the society had become very strong not only in Ashe, Forsyth, and Buncombe counties but in the whole western section of the state.[12]

At the beginning of 1862 there was only a small group in North Carolina ready to make peace at any price and return to the Union; but disaffection was widespread, and for various reasons it continued to increase. In the East, the lack of adequate coast defense and the order to burn cotton to prevent its falling into the hands of the enemy, caused severe and outspoken criticism of the Confederate government. The protection given by the Federals to the people in the territory occupied by the Union troops, made the disloyal there more outspoken and active. The location of a military prison at Salisbury displeased the people in that vicinity, and the disaffection increased as time passed and many North Carolinians were confined there.[13] When the conscription act was passed, disloyalty and disaffection increased rapidly. As before noted, this law did more than any

---

[10] O. R., ser. I, vol. LII, pt. II, pp. 209, 210.
[11] Ibid., p. 232. See above chap. II.
[12] Ibid., p. 210; ser. IV, vol. III, p. 816.
[13] Hamilton, op. cit., p. 44; O. R., ser. IV, vol. II, p. 188.

other one thing to alienate the affections of the common people, whose support was necessary for the success of the Confederacy. It was regarded as a confession that the new government could not depend upon the voluntary support of the people. When they learned of the substitute clause and the nature of the exceptions granted, their complaints grew louder. Prominent men of the state declared that the law was unconstitutional, and that it destroyed public liberty. W. W. Holden, editor of the *Raleigh Standard*, and, as will be noted later, one of the most prominent and active members of the Heroes of America, as well as others who were disloyal to the Confederacy, seized upon the conscription law not only to arouse the disloyal and the indifferent, but also to appeal to the non-slaveholding class and the poorer people. As in other states, the "substitute clause" and the "twenty-negro clause," later known as the "twenty-negro law," were used as arguments to convince both the poor and the non-slaveholders that the great planters were a favored class, that the only issue in the war was the protection of slavery and that the non-slaveholders were to be sacrificed for the benefit of the slave owners. The cry of "a rich man's war and a poor man's fight" was also raised in North Carolina, and it continued there throughout the war. Posing as the representative of the common people, Holden advocated the repeal of both the substitute clause and the "twenty-negro law," and proposed the taxing of land and slaves, in justice to the non-slaveholding class and as a proof that the war was not being fought by the poor for the rich.[14] Holden's criticisms were difficult to meet.

Although many of the non-slaveholding class were willing to fight to maintain slavery because they bitterly opposed Negro equality, which they feared would result from the freeing of the slaves, they objected to the conscription law

[14] Clement Dowd, *Life of Zebulon B. Vance*, pp. 447-48; Stephenson, *The Day of the Confederacy*, pp. 102-3.

because it was a serious question whether or not the families of the mountaineers and of other poor men could manage to survive if all the men of conscription age were taken away from their homes.[15]

The bitter party spirit which developed during 1862 increased the dissatisfaction and disloyalty. Holden and others led an opposition to the Governor, whose policy was "the last man and the last dollar" if necessary to win the war, a policy which did not augur well for those who did not wish to fight and who were working for peace. Holden attacked both the state and the Confederate administrations. Not only did he continue to harp on "a rich man's war and a poor man's fight," but he also brought the charge that the war was being conducted as a "party war," that only strong secessionists and Democrats were allowed to hold office in either the state or the Confederate administration; and he urged that "peace men" be elected to both state and Confederate offices in the August elections. Although Holden advocated Zebulon Vance, who was referred to in the North as the "Northern or Federal candidate," for governor, many believed Holden was paving the way for his own candidacy. Jonathan Worth and Josiah Turner, who opposed the war and were then demanding peace, joined Holden and his followers in supporting Vance for governor against William Johnston, the pro-Davis and Confederate man, who stood for an "unremitting prosecution of the war" and for "no compromise with enemies, traitors, or tories."[16]

The agitation of Holden and his followers soon began to bear fruit. By March, 1862, there were so many de-

---

[15] *O. R.*, ser. I, vol. XVIII, pp. 772-73; ser. IV, vol. II, p. 147.

[16] *A. C.* (1862), pp. 660-61; Ashe, *op. cit.*, II, 714-18, 738; Hamilton, *op. cit.*, p. 41. Vance at this time was colonel of the Twenty-sixth North Carolina regiment. He had been a Whig member of the Thirty-sixth Congress and had opposed secession until Lincoln called for troops. The convention provided for an election for governor and ordered that he begin his term in September instead of the following January. —Hamilton, *op. cit.*, p. 40.

serters in Chatham County that a company had to be sent there to arrest them. But since the criminal code in North Carolina made no provision for the punishment of deserters, it was difficult to do anything with them when caught. Many of the citizens asked that a military court be established in western North Carolina to deal with the disloyal, but this was not done. The statement was constantly made that extreme disloyalty existed in Davidson, Forsyth, Randolph, and Guilford counties. In these counties there was a large Quaker element that opposed the war, not so much because of their objection to the Confederacy as because of their religious beliefs. Some of the men volunteered, but many refused to fight. Deserters, knowing of the sentiment against war in these counties, collected in them in great numbers. Conditions in other counties also caused alarm. In Yadkin and Wilkes the deserters threatened to interfere with the coming elections, and troops were sent to prevent it. In Madison County and farther west, General E. Kirby Smith felt it necessary to send troops to deal with the deserters.[17]

When the election was held, the small vote for Johnston and the "tone and temper of many of the men elected to the General Assembly" indicated the strength of the "peace party" and proved that the enthusiasm for the Confederacy was waning. Vance defeated Johnston almost two to one in the army. In Chatham, Guilford, Randolph, Forsyth, Yadkin, Iredell, and Wilkes counties, where disaffection was prevalent and deserters had collected, Vance received about twenty times as many votes as Johnston. In forty-three of the counties of the state, Vance's majority was more than 19,000.[18]

The policy of Governor Vance and other state officials, in obtaining the release of men accused of disloyalty, gave much aid and encouragement to the disaffected. In De-

[17] Ashe, *op. cit.*, II, 775-76; Hamilton, *op. cit.*, pp. 44-45.
[18] *A. C.* (1862), p. 661; Ashe, *op. cit.*, II, 738.

cember the General Assembly instructed the Governor to demand that Davis return a preacher of Orange County who had been arrested as a spy by the Confederate authorities and imprisoned in Richmond.[19] Not only did they secure the release of this man (against whom the Confederate authorities had found no evidence), but, by the use of the writ of habeas corpus, they also released many North Carolinians who were imprisoned at Salisbury on the charge of disloyalty. Chief Justice Pearson believed that the conscription law was unconstitutional and from this time until the close of the war, there seems to be no record of his having refused a writ of habeas corpus to secure the release of conscripts, deserters, or anyone accused of disloyalty. In May Vance "ordered the militia officers not to arrest persons who had been discharged under writ, and to resist such arrests by persons not authorized by a court having jurisdiction."[20]

When the tax-in-kind and impressment laws were passed in the spring of 1863, Vance, as well as the unionists led by Holden and others, raised the cry that "the Central Government takes our fighting men with one hand and a tenth of our substance with the other."[21] When Major Bradford, of Virginia, was appointed to collect the Confederate tithes in North Carolina, the indignation was so great that Holden felt he dared openly arouse the disloyal and make a definite move for peace.[22]

In the meantime, the disaffection and disloyalty had alarmed Vance so much that he felt something must be done. On January 5, 1863, he wrote the secretary of war that "the impunity which the deserters enjoy and the contagion of their example is operating most ruinously upon the efficiency of the army, to say nothing of the injury to property and citizens." The Governor said that with the occasional assistance of a conscript regiment stationed in that section,

[19] O. R., ser. II, vol. V, pp. 794, 795.
[20] Hamilton, op. cit., pp. 82-84.
[21] A. C. (1863), p. 691.
[22] Hamilton, op. cit., p. 50.

he might be able to make arrests and prevent combinations in the midland and lowland counties, but that he must have Confederate troops to deal with the situation in the mountains where the disloyal from Tennessee had joined the disloyal North Carolinians, and the combined forces had practically stopped all travel and were robbing, burning, and plundering at will.[23]

At this time it was reported that Laurel Valley was filled with tories, and a few days later soldiers had to be sent to Madison County to suppress an outbreak of the disloyal. Some said the reports were exaggerated.

The situation had become such that, on January 26, the Governor issued a proclamation to the absentees in which he asked them to return to their commands and promised to "share the last bushel of meal and pound of meat in the State" with the wives and children of the men in the army.[24] But this failed to produce the desired effect. Three weeks later, in Madison County, when the conscription officers attempted to do their work, there was much trouble. Many of the men "swore that they would die at home before they would be forced off" to the army. When the conscription officers arrived, about one hundred took to the woods, where it was almost impossible to apprehend them because their friends kept them informed of the movements of the conscription officers and the militia. There were so many of the disloyal hid in the woods that they became bold enough to send "menacing messages" to the militia.[25] A short time before, when fourteen loyal men who were sent out to bring in conscripts came upon about two dozen who had taken refuge in a schoolhouse, a skirmish ensued in which two of the best citizens of the county and two of the conscripts were killed.[25a]

[23] *O. R.*, ser. I, vol. XVIII, pp. 821, 822.
[24] *O. R.*, ser. I, vol. XVIII, pp. 810-811, 853-54, 860-61.
[25] *Ibid.*, p. 886.   [25a] *Ibid.*, pp. 880-81.

Although the other conscripts got away, two of them were badly wounded. "In the school-house were found cartridges of the most deadly and murderous quality, made of home-made powder." Although four of the men who were in the fight later came in and surrendered to the officers, "the leaders and the most guilty of them" escaped into the country where the inhabitants readily assisted them in evading the officers.[26]

The citizens were in a quandary as to what to do with the prisoners. If they were tried for murder, it was feared that the Supreme Court would declare the conscription law unconstitutional—in fact, it was said that Judge Pearson was "just itching" for an opportunity to declare it unconstitutional. If this was done, it would justify the men in having resisted the execution of the law, which would make it almost impossible to get another conscript into the army or to keep those who had already been sent. If the men were executed without a trial, which it was feared might happen, that would arouse the disloyal at home and in the army and cause them to wreak vengeance on the loyal citizens.[27]

During the winter of 1863 a disloyal band took charge of Marshall, the county seat of Madison County, and raided the stores. Captain J. A. Keith, Sixty-fourth North Carolina troops, who was sent to deal with them, captured thirteen old men and boys, and ordered them shot. This heartless execution aroused the whole section to white heat. Although Governor Vance requested Secretary Seddon to have Keith dismissed for his brutality, the bitterness of the people remained.[28]

There was also serious trouble in Jackson, Cherokee, and other western counties;[29] and on April 7, the Governor appealed to Secretary Seddon for help against the tories and

[26] *Ibid.*, pp. 880, 886-87.   [27] *Ibid.*, pp. 886-87, 880-81.
[28] Ashe, *op. cit.*, II, 859; O. R., ser. I, vol. XVIII, pp. 880-81, 893, 897, 909.
[29] *Ibid.*, p. 881.

deserters in Yancey, Mitchell, and Watauga counties, where there were so many deserters that the militia could not control them.[30]

Though the Order of the Heroes of America had not yet come to light, reports were being made in 1863 of "the existence of a treasonable society among the North Carolina soldiers in the Army of Northern Virginia," which no doubt was this order.[31]

Disloyalty in the army was so great that the Confederate officers became alarmed. On April 18, 1863, General Lee informed Secretary of War Seddon that there had been "frequent desertions from the North Carolina regiments." Some of the deserters were going home, but the enemy claimed that many were coming to them and giving information. At that time, Lee held six disloyal North Carolinians who had been captured by General D. H. Hill and sent to him. The three that were of conscription age, Lee assigned to North Carolina regiments; but he advised Seddon to send them into the interior, since they would be not only worthless in his army but dangerous. Lee was quite sure they would desert from his own army in Northern Virginia within a week and would carry to the enemy the information that they had collected in North Carolina, Richmond, and elsewhere, as well as any facts concerning the intended movement of his army which they had chanced to hear. The three men over conscription age were sent back to North Carolina with charges against them;[32] but, no doubt, they were released as many others had been.

General Pender reported to Lee at this time that at least two hundred had deserted from the Twenty-fourth North Carolina Regiment in his corps in the last thirty days. Pender attributed the large number of deserters to the actions

[30] Dowd, *op. cit.*, p. 82.
[31] Hamilton, "Heroes of America," *loc. cit.* pp. 10-11.
[32] O. R., ser. I, vol. XVIII, pp. 998, 999.

of Judge Pearson, which had led the men to believe that they would not be molested when they got home. In fact, Sergeant Gross of Pender's Brigade, who had just returned from North Carolina, said that the militia officers in that section told him that they would arrest no more deserters unless protected by a Confederate force. Pender said that the men were constantly receiving letters urging them to leave the army and promising that they would not be molested when they reached home. As a result, men were leaving in squads with their arms. Regiments, Pender said, were being depleted by desertion far more rapidly than they had ever been by battle; and he begged that a force be sent to deal with the disloyal.[33]

The deserters continued to leave in such numbers that in May, 1863, Lee wrote Seddon that the North Carolina troops in his army would soon be greatly reduced unless their desertion could be stopped immediately. During the preceding night, he said, thirty-two men from Company A, Thirty-seventh North Carolina Volunteers, from Ashe County, "deserted, taking with them their arms, equipments, . . . [and] ammunition."[34]

The army officers were aware of Holden's efforts to break down the army and they resented it. On May 9, 1863, General D. H. Hill, who was stationed at Goldsborough, informed Secretary Seddon that there was a powerful faction in North Carolina, poisoning the public mind and looking toward reconstruction. Hill advised the arrest of Holden, who through his paper, the *Standard*, was making the people feel that the war was unjust and that the North Carolina soldiers were treated unfairly by the Confederate government.[35] In June General Hill wrote Seddon that Holden and his followers were "ready to go to

[33] *Ibid.*, p. 998; vol. XXV, pt. II, pp. 746-47.
[34] *Ibid.*, pp. 814-15.
[35] *Ibid.*, vol. XVIII, p. 1053; Ashe, *op. cit.*, II, 835.

Goldsborough to meet the Yankees and welcome them to the state."[36]

After urging the people to hold meetings, Holden through the *Standard* requested them "to cast about and see if negotiations could not be set on foot for an honorable peace." To mislead the loyal who wanted peace but were suspicious of his motives, he stated that "Governor Vance and the editor of the *Standard* are on friendly terms, and we see no reason why we should not remain so."[37] Many of the officials at the capitol were standing by Holden although he was openly denounced as a traitor; and some officials were directly aiding him in arousing the people. Just before the peace meetings began, Jonathan Worth, state treasurer, wrote a friend in Salem that Holden must be sustained and asked the man to secure two hundred subscriptions in Randolph County for the *Standard*. Worth also urged Foster at Thomasville, and Josiah Turner, who was a strong opponent of the "Destructives" as they termed the Confederate supporters, to run for the Confederate Congress.[38]

Since many of the non-slaveholders had shown their willingness to fight to preserve slavery, Holden quoted from the *Progress*, which was the other strong anti-Confederate paper in North Carolina, the following: "We favor peace because we believe that peace now would save slavery, while we very much fear that a prolongation of war will obliterate the last vestige of it."[39] This had the desired effect.

By July, Holden was so actively engaged in peace propaganda that President Davis, who had learned of the peace meetings which were soon to begin, asked Vance if something should not be done to defeat Holden's designs. Vance

[36] *O. R.*, ser. I, vol. XVIII, p. 1092.
[37] Ashe, *North Carolina*, II, 837-38.
[38] *Ibid.*, pp. 838-39.
[39] *Standard*, July 17, 1863. Cited in Hamilton, *Reconstruction in North Carolina*, p. 51.

replied that there was no reconstruction party in North Carolina and that it would be impolitic to take steps against Holden or his paper.[40]

The last of July the Heroes of America started the peace meetings as Holden had planned. In Wake County, where Holden always had a strong personal following, two meetings were held. In each, the Davis administration was condemned, Holden was endorsed, and a demand for peace was made. A few days later, a meeting was held in Surry County in which the people demanded "The Constitution as it is and the Union as it was." Soon other counties followed, some holding two or more meetings. Although similar meetings were held all over the state, most of them were in the central and western parts. Holden said that more than one hundred meetings had been held, and the *Standard* reported the action of sixty which were held in thirty counties. Holden tried to make it appear that the meetings were spontaneous; but Lieutenant George Lay, in reporting the meetings to the Confederate authorities, said that they were "issued from the same mint, the common stamp being that North Carolina has not received due justice or credit, that she has done more than her share, and that her people ought to contribute no further."[41]

When in August, 1863, the Fayetteville *Observer*, a Confederate paper, said that peace meetings were being held by immediate relatives and friends of deserters, or by men who were "screening themselves from obedience to their country's call," in order to countenance the conduct of deserters, and appealed to the *Standard* to discontinue such meetings, Holden declared that the Richmond authorities were trying "to

---

[40] O. R., ser. I, vol. LI, pt. II, pp. 739-40; A. C. (1863), p. 692; Rowland, *Letters and Papers of Jefferson Davis*, V, 577; Hamilton, *op. cit.*, pp. 51-52.

[41] O. R., ser. IV, vol. II, p. 784; Schwab, *Confederate States of America*, pp. 220-21, 201-12, 224-25; Stephenson, *Day of the Confederacy*, p. 170; Hamilton, "Heroes of America," *loc. cit.*, p. 11.

cause a breach between Governor Vance and the great body of his [Holden's] friends in North Carolina," and admonished the conservatives to "stand like a rock. If you give way, all will be lost. The next Congress will sweep away every vestige of civil liberty."[42]

Among loyal soldiers in the army, feeling ran high against Holden because of his treasonable articles in the *Standard* and because of the work of the Order of the Heroes of America. In August, 1863, loyal men in every North Carolina regiment in the Army of Virginia held meetings in which they denounced Holden and appointed delegates to a general convention to be held at Orange Court House, Virginia, on August 12. When the convention met, it issued an address to the people of North Carolina in which it was stated that the disloyal were growing bolder in their statements and acts, which, if not stopped, would lead to civil war. Each criticism of the Davis administration was refuted, and the convention urged the people to support Davis and the war. Though this meeting caused some to withdraw their support from Holden, he continued his work. The *Standard* immediately announced that the Convention at Orange Court House was controlled by officers and that the privates approved of Holden's course. Holden boldly declared that "the Army, as well as the people at home," was with him.[43]

Many of the loyal people of the state now began to demand that Holden's treasonable conduct be stopped. But, knowing that he had a strong personal following near enough to protect him, he announced, in the *Standard* of August 19, that if his enemies dared lift a finger against him, their bodies would be found adorning the trees and lamp posts of Raleigh.[44] On September 7, Governor Vance issued a public proclamation, commanding people to "abstain

[42] Ashe, *op. cit.*, II, 841-42.   [43] *Ibid.*, p. 843.
[44] *Ibid.*, p. 844; *O. R.*, ser. I, vol. LI, pt. II, p. 739.

from assembling for unlawful purposes," and advising them to resort to the ballot box to settle their questions. But Holden persisted. "Let the people speak," he said. "It is refreshing to hear them."[45]

On the night of September 9, 1863, a Georgia regiment, passing through Raleigh, decided to take Holden in hand. Having heard that they were coming, he took refuge in the Governor's mansion. Failing to get him, the soldiers raided the office of the *Standard* and threw the type and some papers into the street. Vance appeared and induced them to disperse. The next morning about seven o'clock the town bell was rung and some two hundred of Holden's followers gathered in the streets of Raleigh. Led by one Mark Williams, a strong Union man, they marched to the office of the *State Journal*, which was the Confederate administration paper, and without interference from either the mayor or police, completely demolished the office. When Vance was notified, he went at once to the scene and prevailed upon the crowd to desist. He then communicated with President Davis, who ordered that troops passing through North Carolina should not enter Raleigh.[46]

But, in spite of this order, on September 11, an Alabama regiment entered the town, and Vance could not control them. In despair, he informed the President of the situation and threatened that, if necessary, he would "recall the North Carolina troops from the field to the defense of their homes."[47]

As a result of the seeming hopelessness of the cause—a hopelessness greatly increased by the outcome of the Battle of Gettysburg and the fall of Vicksburg, many, by the end of the summer of 1863, were demanding peace at any price, while others said, "Peace on any terms that do not degrade us." As early as August 13, Worth had written, " . . . the

[45] Ashe, *op. cit.*, II, 845-46; Hamilton, *Reconstruction in North Carolina*, p. 53.
[46] *Ibid.*, pp. 54-55. [47] Ashe, *op. cit.*, II, 846-47.

masses are determined the war shall cease. As soon as this spirit extends from the people to the Army, the end will come."[48] The Heroes of America were doing all in their power to extend that spirit in the army by writing letters to the soldiers, urging them to come home, and promising them protection when they arrived.[49]

In August, 1863, General Buckner said that "fully half of the East Tennessee and North Carolina troops from the mountain districts are not to be relied upon" and asked to exchange them for others.[50] The following is a part of a letter from a woman living in Madison County to a soldier in the Sixty-fourth North Carolina Volunteers, which Buckner said was a specimen of those received by the North Carolina soldiers. After telling her husband that she had good crops and plenty to eat, she continued:

You said you hadn't anything to eat. I wish you was here to get some beans for dinner. I have plenty to eat as yet. . . . The people is generally well hereat. The people is all turning to Union here since the Yankees has got Vicksburg. I want you to come home as soon as you can after you git this letter. Jane Elkins is living with me yet. That is all I can think of, only I want you to come home the worst that I ever did. The conscripts is all at home yet, and I don't know what they will do with them. The folks is leaving here, and going North as fast as they can. So I will close.

Your wife, till death,
Martha Revis.[51]

Thomas Hunter, who was cutting oats for Mrs. Revis, put in the following:

I pen a line, sir. I am well, and is right strait out for the Union, and I am never going in the service any more, for I am for the Union for ever and ever, amen. I am doing my work.

---
[48] *Ibid.*, pp. 839-40.
[49] *O. R.*, ser. I, vol. XXV, pt. II, pp. 746-47.
[50] *Ibid.*, vol. XXIII, pt. II, p. 950.   [51] *Ibid.*, pp. 950-51.

There was 800 left to go to the North, so will tell you all about it in the next letter; so I will close.

Your brother till death. Hurrah for the Union! Hurrah for the Union, Union!!

Thomas Hunter.[52]

Hunter's letter suggests that he was not only a deserter but that he and Revis were brothers in the Order of the Heroes of America.

General John W. Frazer, who sent this and other similar letters to Buckner and other officers in that section, said that the troops were deserting rapidly and that it was difficult to apprehend them because everyone along the route would feed and harbor them. The last party that Frazer sent out to get deserters had been advised to desert and join the others. At this time, there were 106 of the Sixty-fourth North Carolina Regiment in Madison County without leave. Many were living openly at home and making crops that year.[53] In fact, the whole western part of the state was filled with deserters and men evading the conscription law. Letters were regularly being sent to the army, "stimulating desertion and inviting the men home, and promising them aid and comforts." In the mountains, many had congregated in bands for protection.[54]

It was at this time that deserters with their arms were daily passing through Southwest Virginia on their way to North Carolina. J. E. Joyner, a wounded Confederate on leave in Henry County, Virginia, describes the attitude of these: "When halted and asked for their furloughs or their authority to be absent from their commands, they pat their guns and defiantly say, 'This is my furlough.'" Even the conscription officers turned away "as peaceably as possible" and allowed them to pass on.[55]

[52] *Ibid.*, p. 952.
[53] *Ibid.*, p. 951; ser. IV, vol. II, p. 783.
[54] *Ibid.*, p. 784.
[55] *Ibid.*, p. 721.

In September, 1863, General Preston, superintendent of conscription, was informed that deserters were leaving the army with arms and ammunition and acting in concert to force a passage by bridge, ferry, or any other guarded place.[56]

In central and western North Carolina, the disloyal were organizing into bands of from fifty up to several hundred. In Cherokee County, they captured and assumed a form of military occupation of a town; in Wilkes, five hundred organized into a regiment, intrenched themselves in a camp, and drilled regularly; in Randolph, between three and four hundred organized for resistance. There were also large numbers in Yadkin, Iredell, and Catawba counties. Lieutenant George Lay said that these bands "are not only determined to kill in avoiding apprehension (having just put to death yet another of our enrolling officers), but their esprit de corps extends to killing in revenge as well as in prevention of the capture of each other. So far they seem to have had no trouble for subsistence. While the disaffected feed them from sympathy, the loyal do so from fear."[57] Living up to their obligations in the Order of the Heroes of America, these bands, too, sent letters to the army to get men to desert, and to promise protection to all who would join them.[58]

When the congressional election took place in the fall of 1863, eight of the ten members chosen for the Confederate Congress were "reported to be in favor of peace." George W. Logan, who represented the Tenth District, had been nominated in one of Holden's peace meetings.[59]

[56] *Ibid.*, p. 783.
[57] *Ibid.*, pp. 783-84.   [58] *Ibid.*, pp. 784-85.
[59] Hamilton, *Reconstruction in North Carolina*, p. 55; *A. C.* (1863), p. 692; Stephenson, *op. cit.*, p. 34. The other members elected were: W. H. N. Smith, R. R. Bridgers, Dr. J. T. Leach, Lieutenant Thomas C. Fuller, Captain Josiah Turner, J. A. Gilmer, S. H. Christian, Dr. J. G. Ramsey, B. S. Gaither from the 1st to the 9th districts respectively; *A. C.*, p. 692 (1863). According to Hamilton the successful "peace" candidates were: Leach, Turner, Logan, Christian, and Ramsey.—*Reconstruction in North Carolina*, p. 55.

Although the peace meetings ceased to some extent because of a Confederate force which was sent into the state, desertion from the army continued, some going to the enemy and many going home. Deserters to the enemy, in October, stated that there was much disaffection among North Carolina, Virginia, and Tennessee troops; that Tennesseans were going home in squads every night; and that in some companies, men planned to desert in a body. Two other deserters of the same regiment, which had been stationed in Southwest Virginia until a few days before the Battle of Chattanooga, verified this statement. They also added that the soldiers were quarreling among themselves; that Buckner was liked but both Bragg and Breckenridge were disliked; and that many of the men were convinced that it was "a rich man's war and a poor man's fight." Each of the deserters making statements gave information concerning the numbers, condition, and rations of the Confederate army. They also informed the Federals of the location of guns on Lookout Mountain—the largest of which were "32-pounders"—and of their belief that the Confederates were planning for a flank movement.[60] On October 7, 1863, seven men, one sergeant and six privates, who deserted from the Fifty Kentucky Volunteers were also examined by the Federals. The sergeant said that there was a general feeling of dissatisfaction among the Confederate troops; that he had frequently seen groups of men discussing the question; that eighty from the Sixty-third Tennessee Regiment deserted one night, on the march from Knoxville; that over one hundred had deserted from the Fifty-eighth North Carolina, since the regiment left Loudon; that Georgia troops, according to rumor, had refused to go to the front, and, at least, had not arrived when he left. Then he gave information concerning the Confederate forces and

---

[60] *O. R.*, ser. I, vol. XXX, pt. IV, pp. 179-80.

movements. When the privates were examined, their testimony corroborated the statements of the sergeant.[61]

By the close of 1863, discontent and peace sentiment had become so generally diffused among the people of North Carolina that Vance informed Davis that the discontent could be removed only by an attempt to negotiate with the North, to which Davis replied that it could not be done because of the refusal of the Lincoln government.[62]

By 1864 there were so many deserters in West North Carolina that there was no stigma attached to desertion; and because of the warm welcome accorded them and the safety assured them, deserters not only from North Carolina but from practically every state in the Confederacy, lurked in the mountains and plundered, murdered, or drove out the loyal citizens as they pleased.[63]

Although Vance continued to call on the Secretary of War from time to time to send forces to deal with the disloyal in the state, Judge Pearson, who was believed by some to be a traitor, still held it was no crime to resist arrest for desertion and continued to issue writs of habeas corpus which secured the release of both deserters and conscripts. Vance not only refused to bring any pressure to bear upon the courts, but also declared he was bound by his oath to sustain Pearson and would, if necessary, summon the military force of the state to resist the Confederate States' authorities.[64]

But this very security, which was afforded Holden and the Heroes of America by the state officials, together with their numerical strength, was one of the reasons for their later attempting to elect men who favored peace at any price and who would promise to take North Carolina out of the

[61] *Ibid.*, pp. 181-182.
[62] Hamilton, *Reconstruction in North Carolina*, pp. 55-56.
[63] Stephenson, *op. cit.*, p. 93; *A. C.* (1864), p. 589.
[64] *O. R.*, ser. IV, vol. III, p. 176; Jones, *Diary*, II, 162; Schwab, *op. cit.*, pp. 191-93; Dodd, *op. cit.*, p. 339.

Confederacy, if necessary, and have her, alone, make an attempt to secure peace with Lincoln, provided they did not secure peace before that time. Holden argued that if North Carolina had a right to secede from the United States, she had a right to get out of the Confederacy.[65]

Vance finally felt compelled to sever political relations with Holden. On January 2, 1864, he wrote to D. L. Swain that it was a fixed purpose of Holden and others to call a convention in May to take North Carolina back into the Union and that they had already begun the agitation. A few days before this, resolutions advocating such a course had been prepared in the *Standard* office and sent to Johnston County to be passed at a public meeting to be held in the early part of January; after this January meeting, a series of meetings were to be held all over the state. Senator Pool and Jonathan Worth were two of Holden's right-hand men. Worth said if the people would make known their desire for peace by petition that Vance would "coöperate but otherwise he would not; so day by day, Worth continued to write Anti-secession Whigs trying to get them to demand peace.[66]

Conditions became so serious in North Carolina and some other sections of the Confederacy where secret societies were working, that on February 3, 1864, Davis asked the Confederate Congress for the power to suspend the writ of habeas corpus to cope with the disloyal. He said that he based his request on the facts that "public meetings have been held in some of which a treasonable design is masked by a pretense of devotion to State sovereignty, and in others is openly avowed. . . . A strong suspicion is entertained that secret leagues and associations are being formed. In certain localities men of no mean position do not hesitate to avow their disloyalty and hostility to our cause and their advocacy

---

[65] *A. C.* (1864), p. 589; Schwab, *op. cit.*, p. 222.
[66] Cornelia Phillips Spencer, *Last Ninety Days of War in North Carolina*, pp. 123-24; Ashe, *op. cit.*, II, 868-69; Stephenson, *op. cit.*, p. 171.

of peace, on the terms of submission and the abolition of slavery. In districts overrun by the enemy . . . citizens of well-known disloyalty are holding frequent communication with them, and furnishing valuable information to our enemies, even to the frustration of important military movements." He stated further that though there was good evidence that citizens were disloyal, the civil authorities demanded their release because of lack of legal evidence. Voicing the fear that desertion would become the order of the day, he predicted that unchecked, "bands of deserters will patrol the country, burning, plundering and robbing indiscriminately, and our armies, already too weak, must be still further depleted at the most imminent crisis of our cause, to keep the peace and protect the lives and property of our citizens at home."[67]

On February 24, the *Standard* announced the passing of the act of Congress suspending the writ of habeas corpus. The same issue also announced that the publication of the *Standard* would be suspended indefinitely.[68]

On March 3 Holden announced that he would be a candidate for governor, against Vance. Holden said the issue was "war or peace" and he stood for peace. Both of the candidates were peace men but Vance stood for an attempt to make peace by acting "in coöperation with the other Confederate States," while Holden advocated a separate peace and was "stigmatized as 'the peace-at-any-price' candidate.' "[69]

In the meantime, the meeting in Johnston County had been held and the resolutions setting forth the need of a convention to discuss peace, which Dr. J. T. Leach and Holden had prepared, were introduced into the meeting by

[67] Dodd, *Jefferson Davis*, pp. 323-24; Rowland, *Jefferson Davis, Constitutionalist*, VI, 165-6; Stephenson, *op. cit.*, pp. 119-21.
[68] Hamilton, *Reconstruction in North Carolina*, p. 59.
[69] *A. C.* (1864), p. 589; Stephenson, *op. cit.*, pp. 170-71; Ashe, *op. cit.*, II, 879; Hamilton, *Reconstruction in North Carolina*, p. 59; Dowd, *op. cit.*, p. 165.

Leach as had been planned. Other meetings of the same nature followed and the proceedings of about thirty were published. Every one expressed hostility to the Confederate government and practically demanded peace.[70]

Since it was several months before the election, each side began to cast about for campaign material. Early in the campaign some of Vance's supporters said Holden was connected with a treasonable society; but since this was one of the favorite devices for injuring one's political opponents, not much attention was paid to it by the public. But on July 6, 1864, the "Conservatives," supporting Vance, published a full account of the Order of the Heroes of America, accompanied by a signed confession from the Reverend Orin Churchill, of Caswell County, who had joined the society.[71]

Soon confessions were made by many men who claimed that they did not mean to be disloyal but that they had been induced to join the order because they wanted protection for themselves, but particularly for their families, from the Federals in case the latter invaded North Carolina. Most of the men withdrawing from the society said that they had been induced to join by a member whom they considered a friend. They had been told that the organization would furnish them certain information useful to them and their families in case the Federals overran their section. No one had told them that, when they were members, they were supposed to give information to the Federals in return for the protection promised. Neither did they understand that, in order to receive the information and aid promised, the Federals must in some way be connected with the society so as to be able to respond to the appeal for help and protection. Some of the members claimed they were not told, even after they joined, that they must give information to the enemy and work

---

[70] Hamilton, *Reconstruction in North Carolina*, p. 57 n.

[71] Hamilton, "Heroes of America," *loc. cit.*, pp. 11-12; Hamilton, *Reconstruction in North Carolina*, p. 61.

against the Confederacy. This probably was true, because the leaders and other disloyal members were using the society to secure votes for the "peace men" in the fall elections.[72]

Eleven men who made affidavits before D. W. Gibson, who was acting justice of the peace of Richmond County, stated that about the last of May, 1864, a Mr. Phillips, of Randolph County, appeared in their neighborhood and "introduced what he called a good society which originated with the Yankees and was communicated to our people by a surgeon named Johnson." Phillips told them that "the object of the society was to afford protection to our lives and property, in case our section should be overrun by the Yankees." After the men were initiated, they were further told that the enemy was "disposed to favor all good Conservative men, and that this was the means by which ... [the Federals] would know them"; that in case of raids or subjugation, "we would not be hurt or even in the event of capture that the Yankees would release us, treat us well, etc." These men also claimed that members did not really know what the society was until they were initiated and then it was too late.[73]

Practically all of the men who confessed that they were members said that most of the branches of the order had been instructed to vote for Holden in the August election because he was a member and in complete sympathy with the society; that he was a good conservative; that the Federals favored conservatives and that this was the way they had of knowing the members of the society. Professor Hamilton says that a living member whom he interviewed assured him that this was generally the case.[74]

The exposure of the society and its treasonable purposes lost Holden many votes. He was not only a member of the

[72] Hamilton, "Heroes of America," *loc. cit.*, pp. 12-14; Hamilton, *Reconstruction in North Carolina*, p. 62.

[73] Hamilton, "Heroes of America," *loc. cit.*, pp. 13-14. The names of the men making these statements may be found on p. 13.

[74] *Ibid.*, p. 14; Hamilton, *Reconstruction in North Carolina*, p. 64.

organization but he was also accused of being in the pay of the North—an accusation which many believed. Although he ridiculed the idea of the existence of such an organization, facts were facts and he could not get around them. While all of the conservatives had been in sympathy with his plans for peace, the loyal element naturally turned against him; and, no doubt, many of the disloyal refrained from voting for him both because of the stigma attached to such action and because they feared discovery. When the election was held in the army, Vance received 13,209 out of the 15,033 votes cast, which would seem to indicate that the Heroes of America had only a few members in the army.[75] But, as before stated, any soldier knew that he would be suspected of being disloyal if it were known that he had voted for Holden, after it had been disclosed that Holden was a member of the Heroes of America. Moreover, Vance had gone to Lee's army, previous to the election, and made strong appeals to the soldiers to support him and to defeat Holden because of the latter's treasonable designs. Out of 892 votes cast by soldiers in the hospitals of Richmond, only twenty-five were cast for Holden. In one hospital where there were 355 votes cast, only one was for Holden; and it was said that the man who voted for him was crazy. The *Greensborough Patriot* said that Holden would have received more votes if he had had ballot boxes put in the woods where most of his military supporters were hiding.[76] In the vote in the state, which followed that of the army, Holden carried only Randolph and Johnston counties.[77]

Holden made accusations of fraud and intimidation in the election but did not press his charges. Professor Hamilton says that examination of the records shows no fraud,

---

[75] *A. C.* (1864), p. 589; Ashe, *op. cit.*, II, 921-22; Hamilton, *Reconstruction in North Carolina*, p. 64.
[76] *A. C.* (1864), p. 589; Hamilton, *Reconstruction in North Carolina*, p. 64.
[77] *Ibid.*

but that "without question, voting for Holden subjected one to violent unpopularity."[78]

Immediately after the election, Holden, through his paper, declared himself to be a friend to both the state and Confederate governments and in favor of a vigorous prosecution of the war, but in favor also of every effort to make peace on honorable terms.[79] This was only for effect: Bartholomew F. Moore, a lawyer of Raleigh who was a strong unionist and who testified after the war that he had secured the release, by the use of the writ of habeas corpus, of many members of the Order of the Heroes of America, said he knew that Holden never favored the Confederacy but favored reconstruction throughout the entire war, because Holden often talked to him during the war about restoring North Carolina to the Union.[80]

Although members of the organization were tried in the courts for treason, there seems to be no record that any of them were punished. Immediately after the existence of the order was made known, several in Wake County were arrested and brought before the justice of the peace for trial. B. E. Moore, an ardent Mason and unionist, defended them. His plea was that the purposes of the society were no more treasonable than the purposes of Masonry. The men were released.[81]

Loyal Masons bitterly resented Moore's charge, and immediately in July, 1864, Columbus Lodge No. 102 at Pittsboro, North Carolina, passed resolutions stating that Moore and the *Progress* were attempting to connect the Heroes of America with Masonry; that the lodge not only denounced any connection with the order but severely condemned it and would promptly expel any Mason found to be connected with it.[82]

[78] *Ibid.*, p. 64 n.   [79] *Ibid.*, pp. 64-65.
[80] *Senate Report*, 1st Session, 42nd Cong., pp. 199, 208.
[81] Hamilton, "Heroes of America," *loc. cit.*, p. 14.   [82] *Ibid.*

Although the Order of the Heroes of America was known to be a treasonable society, it continued throughout the war and its members were in constant communication with the North.[83] J. L. Johnson, of Forsyth County, went to Washington during the war and initiated into the society President Lincoln, General Grant, Professor Benjamin S. Hedrick, Mr. Barrett, commissioner of pensions, and others.[84] Evidently this was done to give the society prestige at home, and not only to assure the members that the North approved of it and would give them protection in case of an invasion, but also, perhaps, to encourage the ignorant to join in hopes of getting a pension after the war and thus to substantiate the statement that they should share in the division of the property of loyal Confederates, which would be made after the war. Moreover, when Federal officers came among the disloyal to organize them, the disloyal were more susceptible to the enemies' suggestions.[85]

By the fall of 1864, depression was widespread among the people of North Carolina. Practically all of the men of conscription age were away from home—the loyal in the army and the disloyal either in the army or in hiding. In the central counties and in the mountains, there were not only the disloyal from North Carolina but also many from South Carolina, Georgia, and Tennessee. In some communities they had succeeded in driving out all of the people who were in sympathy with the Confederacy. Federal officers went among them persuading them to ally themselves with the Union forces, and advising them as to what course to pursue. General Sherman and General Schofield encouraged Colonel G. W. Kirk, a Federal officer in this region, to organize the disloyal men in the mountains rather than to undertake

[83] In fact, it changed its purpose and continued through the Reconstruction Period. Hamilton, "Heroes of America," *loc. cit.*, p. 14; Fleming, *Sequel of Appomattox*, pp. 179, 245.
[84] Testimony of Daniel R. Goodloe, cited above, p. 33 n.
[85] Cf. p. 33, above.

hazardous expeditions against the enemy. They insisted that he organize "the element in North Carolina hostile to Jeff. Davis into a series of scouting companies, who would protect each other, interrupt as much as possible the communications of the enemy, destroy his [the Confederates'] supply depots, and bring in such information as may be useful to us [the Federals]." They offered to give Kirk any assistance they could in carrying out such a project.[86]

Some of the Confederate officers in the western section of North Carolina were disloyal, which made the situation more difficult to deal with. Seddon, writing to Vance in December, 1864, regarding the "mountain country of Western North Carolina," called to the Governor's attention the fact that Colonel Thomas's command was a favorite resort of deserters. Thomas was disobedient to Confederate orders and invariably avoided the enemy when his command advanced.[87]

The new year of 1865 dawned with the central and western part of the state filled with bands of deserters, and the people clamoring for peace. There was no abatement in the disloyalty before the close of the war.[88] This state of affairs leads one to believe that Linville Price, a deserter from the Thirty-fourth North Carolina regiment from Ashe County, and E. B. Petrie, of Forsyth County, two members of the Order of the Heroes of America, spoke truly when they said that "the order was extensive" in their section of the state.[89]

SOUTH CAROLINA

In South Carolina an organization was found to exist among the disloyal in some of the counties which bordered parts of North Carolina in which the Order of the Heroes of America was very strong.

[86] *O. R.*, ser. I, vol. XXXIX, pt. I, pp. 232-34; vol. XLII, pt. III, p. 1251.
[87] *Ibid.*, ser. I, vol. XLII, pt. III, p. 1253.
[88] *Ibid.*, vol. XLVII, pt. II, pp. 1250-55.
[89] *Ibid.*, ser. IV, vol. III, p. 816.

During the first year of the war, there seem to have been no unionists nor any disaffection in South Carolina. Even the most ignorant mountaineers, who were not much concerned with the struggle, volunteered and furnished some of the best corps in service from South Carolina.[90] But by the spring of 1862, disaffection appeared among the troops at Fort Sumter, and prominent citizens of Charleston reported to Major Pemberton and James Chesnut, Jr., that disaffection prevailed to such an extent in the garrison at Fort Sumter that the troops had threatened to mutiny and to refuse to fire on the enemy should one appear.[91] Upon investigation, Major Pemberton arrested one man because he had used seditious language in the presence of a citizen of Charleston, and ordered him tried before a court-martial; but Pemberton said that there was no more disaffection among the troops than would be found in most corps in the Confederate service.[92] However, immediately following this reassurance, five men deserted and some of the guns were spiked; and F. W. Pickens, from the military headquarters in South Carolina, requested Pemberton to send certain companies to Charleston to restore confidence in the garrison.[93]

It was thought that the trouble was caused by men whose term of service had almost expired, but who would be compelled to remain in service because of the conscription act. They no doubt were encouraged to cause trouble because Rhett and other prominent South Carolinians were criticizing the conscription law and doing all they could to bring Davis into disrepute. Rhett even went so far as to suggest impeachment to get rid of Davis.[94] Mrs. Chesnut said she did not know a half-dozen men in Columbia, South Carolina, "who would not gaily step into Jeff Davis's shoes with a firm conviction that they would do better in every respect than

---

[90] *Ibid.*, vol. II, p. 769.
[91] *Ibid.*, ser. I, vol. XIV, p. 508.
[92] *Ibid.*, pp. 517, 518.
[93] *Ibid.*, pp. 515, 517.
[94] Dodd, *Jefferson Davis*, p. 300.

he does";[95] and that "from the poor old blind bishop downward everybody is besetting him [Mr. Chesnut] to let off students, theological and others from going into the army."[96]

Rumors of disloyalty at Fort Sumter continued. In June, 1862, Colonel Calhoun, being aware not only of the rumors of disloyalty but also of the seditious language of some of the garrison, made an investigation. The company officers did not believe their men were disloyal and some of the officers asked to be transferred to the West or to Virginia to stop the rumors of what they considered an overanxious community.[97]

Pemberton refused to remove any of the troops from Charleston, though he admitted some were disloyal.[98] Throughout the next year, the charges of disloyalty at Fort Sumter continued.

By 1863, many soldiers in South Carolina had become weary of war. Their families were suffering, and, believing the cause of the South was lost, they refused to support the war any longer. John D. Ashmore, chief enrolling officer of the Fifth Congressional District of South Carolina, wrote on August 7 that men at home refused to enter the army, and many in the army deserted and came home. Both of these classes were sustained in their conduct by many of the people in their section, a few of whom were citizens of property and social position who up to 1863 had been regarded as "good and loyal citizens." Some of these now proclaimed hostility to the southern cause and not only countenanced the disloyal, but advised and induced men to desert; while others said that the cause was lost and, like the people of other sections, urged that the war be stopped.[99]

By the summer of 1863 large bands of deserters and

[95] *Diary*, p. 140.
[96] *Ibid.*, p. 141.
[97] *O. R.*, ser. I, vol. XIV, pp. 562-63, 564-565.
[98] *Ibid.*, p. 527.
[99] *Ibid.*, ser. IV, vol. II, pp. 771-72.

renegade conscripts had taken refuge in the mountains of Greenville, Pickens, and Spartanburg counties, and much disaffection existed among the people in that section of the state.[100] Major C. D. Melton, commandant of conscripts of South Carolina, thought the disaffection was almost wholly confined "to the mountainous portions of those districts along the North Carolina line."[101] These people were not unionists; and it will be recalled that these very localities which were infested with deserters and other disaffected people had furnished some of the best companies in service from South Carolina during the early part of the war.

Major Melton further stated that the disaffected in these regions banded together for definite purposes and had leaders, spies, and signals of distress and danger.[102] Captain Southern reported on August 17 that they had elected officers and were regularly organized in the mountains; and that "every woman, and child is a watch and a guard for them."[103]

The bands were composed of ten, twenty, or thirty conscripts and deserters whose chief aim was to prevent capture and return to the army. "They swear by all they hold sacred that they will die at home before they will ever be dragged forth again to do battle for such a cause."[104] They also encouraged all conscripts at home to join them; and the men in the disloyal bands and other disaffected people, by writing letters to soldiers in the army from that section, giving deplorable pictures of the destitution of their families, encouraged soldiers to desert and join them.[105]

In both Pickens and Greenville counties, these bands had definite meeting places. The more important meeting places in Pickens were "the mouth of Brasstown Creek on Tugaloo; the passes west and northwest of Tunnel Hill, Cherokee,

[100] *Ibid.*, pp. 769-70, 771, 772, 773.
[101] *Ibid.*, p. 769.
[102] *Ibid.*, pp. 770, 771.
[103] *Ibid.*, p. 774.
[104] *Ibid.*, p. 772.
[105] *Ibid.*, pp. 770, 769.

bordering the Jocassee Valley; and Table Rock."[106] A deserter's cabin was located in almost every intermediate pass and valley. Whenever a stranger approached, the men of the home would hide among the rocks and ravines, perhaps in a place where they could observe all that went on. They remained in hiding until informed by the children or women of the household that it was safe to return home. In Greenville County, their chief meeting places were at "Caesar's Head, Potts' Cove, Solomon's Jaws, Turnpike, Saluda Gap, on the headwaters of the Tyger, Howard's Gap, and Hogback Mountain, as well as all intermediate points."[107]

Northeast of Greenville Courthouse in the vicinity of Greenville, a heavy log building had been loop-holed and prepared for defense. Major C. D. Melton was informed by John D. Ashmore of his plan to obtain a "swivel or 6 pounder to demolish a blockhouse."[108] Ashmore thought the destruction of it would prevent much bloodshed in future and also alarm the bands and cause them to return to duty.[109]

In Spartanburg County, the disloyal had no regular meeting places. They lived in their farmhouses in the valley and on the hills, and "by a well-arranged system of signals give warning of the approach of danger."[110] Several bands joined and engaged in farming and making liquor; some even traveled about the country with a threshing machine. Part of the men would watch while the others worked.[111]

On August 16, 1863, Major Ashmore reported that a number of deserters had arrived the previous week from the Twenty-second South Carolina Regiment, which was at Augusta.[112]

Major Melton reported on August 25, 1863, that the Sixteenth South Carolina Volunteer Regiment of General

[106] *Ibid.*, p. 772.
[107] *Ibid.*
[108] *Ibid.*, p. 773.
[109] *Ibid.*
[110] *Ibid.*, p. 772.
[111] *Ibid.*, p. 773.
[112] *Ibid.*

Evans' brigade, which was made up almost entirely of companies from Greenville, Pickens, and Spartanburg counties, had arrived and joined the deserters. This regiment had been in service for about two years. After finishing an arduous campaign in North Carolina, they had been sent to Charleston, where they hoped to stay. When they were ordered to go to Jackson, most of them took their arms and went home; perhaps they intended to make only a short visit, but when they got there, being tired of war and encouraged by the home people and the disloyal bands to remain, they did so.[113]

Soon afterward, men from other regiments began to go home. It became quite common to see squads of ten or fifteen come walking home with their arms. Many from General Clingman's brigade across the line in North Carolina joined them.[114]

These bands became a terror to the loyal citizens and a menace to the Confederacy. They not only destroyed the property of the loyal citizens and threatened them with violence, but they also threatened to bring in the enemy to invade that section. The loyal people were afraid to engage in service to arrest them because the disloyal had threatened them with the knife and torch if they attempted to make any arrests. Major Ashmore asked for soldiers from a distance to aid him in suppressing them. He attempted to get in touch with the leaders but failed. Learning from the conscript agents that there were several hundred more, he made an earnest appeal to them to return to their duty. Four or five returned but the others only showed ridicule and contempt for him.[115]

The situation was exceedingly hard to deal with because of the inaccessibility of the mountains, the perfect organization of the bands, and the disaffection of the people in gen-

[113] *Ibid.,* p. 769.
[114] *Ibid.,* p. 770.   [115] *Ibid.,* p. 771.

eral. Melton reported as early as August, 1863, that in the northwestern section of the state, it was "no longer a reproach to be known as a deserter"; that all were ready to encourage and aid the efforts of those who were avoiding military duty; that no one would give information. In fact, there were but few families in the section that had not a father, husband, son, brother, or some other kinsman, a deserter in the mountains.[116]

Conditions reached such a state that the governor of South Carolina not only sent troops to be used in suppressing the disloyalty in Northwest South Carolina, but also asked Governor Vance of North Carolina to send forces to the North Carolina side to act in concert with the forces from South Carolina.[117]

Disloyalty to the Confederacy, both in the army and at home, continued in South Carolina throughout the war. On January 31, 1864, Colonel W. W. H. Davis, of the Union army, reported that three deserters came within his lines at Morris Island, South Carolina, and gave him a full description of conditions in Charleston, of the Confederate army on James Island, and of the dissatisfaction in its ranks. Not only privates but also some of the officers were anxious to quit the Confederate service. Sixteen of the company to which the deserters belonged had deserted to the Federals on January 30.[118] There was still much disaffection in the Twenty-second South Carolina Regiment, and the deserters reported that disloyal officers in the regiment were making light of the suspected disaffection in order to shield their men. Many of the men in the First Regiment of South Carolina Infantry were not disloyal to the South but were dissatisfied because they believed their term of enlistment had expired,[119] and they wished to go home.

[116] *O. R., Ibid.*, p. 769. [117] *Ibid.*, p. 770.
[118] *Ibid.*, ser. I, vol. XXXV, pt. I, p. 462.
[119] *Ibid.*, p. 518.

In the southeastern corner of the state, in the region near Beaufort, in which the Federals had control, a mass state convention was held on April 17, 1864. "The call for the Convention invited the people of the State 'without distinction of color' to participate in the election of delegates to the Baltimore Presidential Convention. About one hundred and fifty colored persons and two-thirds as many whites assembled and selected twelve whites and four Africans as delegates."[120]

Although the secession state government controlled most of the state and Governor Bonham and also Governor Magrath, who succeeded him, declared they would consider no peace without independence,[121] the state government never succeeded in stamping out disaffection.

[120] *A. C.* (1864), p. 752.   [121] *Ibid.*, pp. 752, 743.

CHAPTER VII

UNIONISM IN EAST TENNESSEE AND SOUTHWEST VIRGINIA

EAST TENNESSEE

FROM one point of view, the East Tennesseans should not be included in the present study, because the majority of them opposed withdrawing from the Union in 1861 and many of them never pretended to support the Confederacy at any time during its existence.[1] But because the state of Tennessee did secede from the Union and the East Tennesseans were, therefore, in territory claimed by the Confederacy and, until the Federals gained control of the state in 1862, were ruled by a government loyal to the Confederacy,[2] it seems necessary to the completeness of the present survey, to include them. Moreover, a study of the opposition to the Confederacy in this large block of territory is another important evidence that the Confederacy did not have the support of all that were considered its citizens and were counted upon to give it their aid.

It is, of course, to be expected that in East Tennessee we should find, from the outset, much secret and some open and avowed hostility to the Confederacy, with many of the disaffected taking refuge in the mountains of the region during the war.[3] By June, 1861, a number of Union companies had been formed in the disaffected districts, and they were "drilling daily for the avowed purpose of resistance."[4] Be-

[1] DeLeon, *Four Years in Rebel Capitals*, pp. 182-83; Humes, *The Loyal Mountaineers of Tennessee*, pp. 7, 9.

[2] *Parson Brownlow's Book*, pp. 139, 210, 220-23; Temple, *East Tennessee and the Civil War*, pp. 162, 366, *et passim*.

[3] O. R., ser. I, vol. IV, pp. 393, 366, *et passim.* Stephenson, *The Day of the Confederacy*, p. 165.

[4] O. R., ser. I, vol. LII, pt. II, p. 116.

cause of the Union sympathies of the people, a Federal army could move without interference from the Georgia line to Cumberland Gap. On June 7 an alarm was given in Bradley County that the Confederates were coming to disarm all unionists. This, though false, revealed a complete organization of the unionists. In twelve hours this organization assembled about one thousand men at previously designated rendezvous.[5] Temple says that the unionists would have remained quietly at home and caused no trouble had they not been mistreated by the ardent Confederates and required to fight for the Confederacy.[6] After the Battle of Bull Run, feeling ran high and the unionists were taunted with being "Lincolnites," "tories," and cowards. About this time, T. A. R. Nelson, Horace Maynard, and other Union leaders started north, while many Union sympathizers began to pour into Kentucky, some to remain as refugees, others to join the Federal army and return to Tennessee to wreak vengeance on the Confederates.[7]

Although the Confederate authorities strictly enjoined "the most scrupulous regard for the personal property rights of all of the inhabitants" and encouraged the return of the people who had fled from their homes under apprehension of danger, the exodus of the unionists continued, and a reign of terror began.[8] To prevent the unionists from having uninterrupted communication with the Federals, the passes through the mountains from the base of the Blue Ridge in Virginia to the slope of the Cumberlands in Middle Tennessee were picketed by Confederate soldiers. Despite this fact, many of those opposing the Confederacy went through unknown passes or slipped by the guards while they dozed.

[5] *Ibid.*, vol. IV, pp. 367, 366; ser. II, vol. I, pp. 828, 829.
[6] Temple, *East Tennessee and the Civil War*, pp. 366-67.
[7] *O. R.*, ser. II, vol. I, p. 837; Humes, *op. cit.*, pp. 158-159; Temple, *op. cit.*, p. 367.
[8] *Ibid.*, p. 369.

The bitterness of the unionists was increased when they learned that the Confederate soldiers were stationed at the passes solely to prevent them from leaving Tennessee and escaping the punishment which the Confederates intended to visit on them.[9] As a result, the property and life of loyal Confederates were so endangered by the unionists that in October a large group of loyal Confederates appealed to Governor Harris for protection. Renegade Tennesseans, they said, were acting as pickets for the Federal army at Albany, Kentucky, which is about six miles from the Tennessee line, and were leading hostile bands against the loyal Confederate citizens. The leader of these bands was thought to be the "notorious Jim Ferguson," the murderer of several Confederates. His ambition seemed "to be to shoot Southern men in cold blood" wherever he found them; and he was at that time "seeking to shoot his own brother because he is in the [Confederate] army here." Ferguson had placed the names of many Confederates on the "black list," which meant that they were to be killed and their property destroyed.[10]

It will be recalled that by November so many of the unionists in East Tennessee had crossed into North Carolina and had become such a menace to the life and property of loyal Confederates there that Governor Brown, of Georgia, and Governor Clark, of North Carolina, had appealed to Secretary Benjamin to send troops to suppress the treason in that section. Moreover, Governor Clark said he feared that not only would some of the North Carolinians "be somewhat affected by the superiority [in numbers] of the traitors or their artful promises," but also that the lead mines, salt-works, and railroads in that section would be endangered by the traitors.[11]

[9] *O. R.*, ser. I, vol. LII, pt. II, p. 180; Temple, *op. cit.*, pp. 369-70.
[10] *O. R.*, ser. I, vol. LII, pt. II, pp. 178-80.
[11] *Ibid.*, pp. 209-10.

Governor Clark's fears were not unfounded. Indeed, William Blount Carter, an active Union leader, was at that time in Washington in conference with Lincoln, Seward, and McClellan, suggesting to them a "simultaneous destruction of all the bridges on the East Tennessee and Georgia Railroad and on the East Tennessee and Virginia road, between Bridgeport and Bristol, a distance of 270 miles, and also a long bridge over the Tennessee at Bridgeport, Alabama, on the Memphis and Charleston road." At the time the bridges, nine in number, were to be burned, a Federal army was to invade East Tennessee and the unionists were to rise in rebellion against the Confederacy and join the Federals. Lincoln and McClellan expressed their approval of Carter's scheme by giving him "$2,500 with which to secure the destruction of the bridges" and promising to send the army. The roads in question were deemed vital to the Confederate cause because they brought supplies and troops to the army in Virginia.[12] November 8, 1861, was selected as the day to burn the bridges. In accordance with carefully prepared plans, on that day attempts were made to demolish them. The unionists succeeded in destroying five out of nine and cut the telegraph wires at various places between Knoxville and Chattanooga and between Knoxville and Bristol;[13] but much to their disappointment, the Federal expedition into East Tennessee which they were expecting at this time, was postponed.

Despite the fact that Carter worked so cautiously that the bridge-burners were not at the time suspected even by their closest neighbors,[14] his scheme hurt the unionist cause far more than it did the Confederate cause, for it alarmed the Confederates and aroused a bitter feeling toward the union-

---

[12] Temple, *op. cit.*, pp. 370-71, 378-79; DeLeon, *op. cit.*, pp. 182-83; *A. C.* (1861), p. 685; *Natchez Courier*, Jan. 25, 1862.

[13] *A. C.* (1861), p. 685; *Parson Brownlow's Book*, pp. 264-65; O. R., ser. II, vol. I, pp. 838, 839, 840, 841, 843; Temple, *op. cit.*, pp. 376, 378-79.

[14] *Ibid.*, pp. 379-80.

ists, whereas the actual burning of the bridges injured the Confederacy but little. When it was found that many were in arms and were rising or ready to rise against the Confederacy,[15] the Confederates were angered and decided that the unionists must be dealt with severely. As a result, the prisons were soon filled. Many of the less prominent unionists were imprisoned in Tennessee, while those considered more dangerous were sent to Mobile and Tuscaloosa, Alabama, Macon, Georgia, and other places in the lower South.[16]

Confederate forces were sent to quell the rebellion which followed and to capture the bridge-burners if possible. On November 11, R. L. Owen, the president of the Virginia and Tennessee Railroad, reported to Secretary Benjamin that about four hundred unionists were in camp at N. G. Taylor's, about five miles from Bristol, and that it was reported that five hundred more were encamped two miles from Taylor's; that reënforcements were constantly reaching them from Watauga County, North Carolina, and from Johnson, Carter, and Washington counties in Tennessee. President Owen was sure these counties could furnish two thousand unionists.[17] The same day Colonel W. B. Wood of Knoxville wrote General Cooper that the whole country was in a state of rebellion; that a thousand men were within six miles of Strawberry Plains Bridge and he contemplated an attack the next day; that five hundred had that day left Hamilton County and had gone toward Loudon Bridge; that the Confederates repelled an attack made on Watauga the day before, but that the unionists were gathering more men and he feared they would renew the attack when better organized; that another camp was being formed in Sevier County and

[15] O. R., ser. II, vol. I, pp. 837, 835.
[16] Temple, op. cit., pp. 387, 406, 407, 408; *Parson Brownlow's Book*, p. 266; O. R., ser. II, vol. I, p. 835.
[17] Ibid., p. 839.

three hundred men had arrived and more were coming all the time from Blount, Roane, Johnson, Greene, Carter, and other counties; and that the loyal Confederate citizens were so alarmed in certain communities that they were moving their families to places of safety and would gladly enlist in the Confederate army if he had arms for them. Because of the pressing need, Colonel Wood ordered all of the arms in Knoxville seized and authorized Major Campbell to impress all he could find in the hands of the Union men, who, he thought, ought to be regarded as avowed enemies.[18] During the next three weeks, many other similar reports, which showed the uprising of the unionists to be general, came from both Confederate officers and loyal Confederate citizens.[19]

Since the Federal army did not come to the aid of the unionists as promised, the Confederate troops were successful in breaking up many of the camps, capturing large numbers of men, and suppressing the rebellion.[20] Many, to escape arrest and capture, either fled to the mountains or took the oath of allegiance to the Confederate government.[21] Since most of the people were Union sympathizers, it was a question what to do with them. The prisons were soon filled. Colonel W. B. Wood in his report to the Secretary of War following the capture of a group of unionists, suggested that "to release them is ruinous; to convict them before a court at this time next to an impossibility; but if they are kept in prison for six months it will have a good effect."[22] The prisoners told the Confederates that when they rebelled they had been assured by their leaders that the Federals were in the state and would join them in a few days. Secretary Ben-

---

[18] *Ibid.*, p. 840.

[19] *Ibid.*, pp. 841-42, 843, 844, *et passim.*.

[20] See *ibid.*, pp. 829-912 for a full account of the revolt of the East Tennesseans and the suppression of it by the Confederates.

[21] O. R., ser. II, vol. I, p. 848; Temple, *op. cit.*, pp. 402-3.

[22] O. R., ser. II, vol. I, p. 846.

jamin decided that "all such as can be identified as having been engaged in bridge-burning" who had been captured should be hanged; that all men known to have been up in arms against the Confederacy should be held in jail as prisoners of war during the remainder of the war; and that those who voluntarily surrendered themselves and their arms should be allowed to take the oath of allegiance to the Confederacy and return to their homes.[23]

Besides "Parson" Brownlow, Horace Maynard, and T. A. R. Nelson, who were avowed and outspoken unionist leaders, there were many prominent men who secretly used their wealth in the Union cause. Though this latter class of leaders managed not to be found actually in arms, they did more damage to the Confederacy in East Tennessee than the men who were thus discovered. Colonel Wood, in a letter to Secretary Benjamin on November 20, places in this class "Judge [David T.] Patterson, the son-in-law of Andrew Johnson; Colonel [Samuel] Pickens, the senator in the legislature from Sevier and other counties, and several members of the legislature, besides others of influence and some distinction in their counties."[24] Practically all of the Union leaders were Whigs.[25] Although many of the leaders were, as before stated, not found in arms, the Confederate officers had them arrested; and Benjamin on November 25, 1861, ordered them sent to Tuscaloosa, Alabama, to be imprisoned until the close of the war. Among those sent, were Judge Patterson, Senator Pickens, and "Parson" Brownlow.[26]

By the close of the year, the rebellion against the Confederacy was suppressed, but the unionists had by no means become loyal Confederates. Although many took the oath of

[23] *Ibid.*, p. 848; Temple, *op. cit.*, pp. 403-13.
[24] *O. R.*, ser. II, vol. I, p. 845; *Parson Brownlow's Book*, p. 267; *O. R.*, ser. I, vol. III, pt. II, p. 116.
[25] Temple, *op. cit.*, p. 219.
[26] *O. R.*, ser. I, vol. LII, pt. II, p. 232; *Tribune Almanac* (1862), p. 46; *Parson Brownlow's Book*, pp. 267-68, 270; Temple, *op. cit.*, pp. 390-92.

allegiance to the Confederate government and seemed submissive, they secretly continued to sympathize with the Federals and at the "first intimation that the Lincoln army was like to penetrate the state they were in arms ... and ready to join them and make war upon us."[27] Reports show that the unionists were organizing to protect themselves and to cause trouble for the Confederacy. As noted in connection with North Carolina, in the early part of December, 1861, Brigadier General W. H. Carroll informed General A. S. Johnston that an effort was on foot for a thorough organization of the disloyal in East Tennessee and the border counties of North Carolina, and asked for more arms to meet the situation.[28] It may have been at this time that the Order of the Heroes of America was organized. A few days later, Carroll again reported that "recreant Tennesseans with a few miscreants from other states were organizing themselves into predatory bands in the counties of Blount, Sevier, Cocke, Hancock, Scott, Campbell, and other counties bordering on the North Carolina and Kentucky line."[29]

Since the Confederate government in Tennessee collapsed in 1862, the unionists and others who were not in sympathy with the Confederacy found it comparatively easy, from that time on, to give aid to the Union and to work against the Confederacy.

When the first conscription law was passed, there was such an exodus of the unionists to the mountains of East Tennessee and the neighboring states that men known as guides or "pilots" spent their time in conducting parties of refugees through the woods and mountains to places of safety, or to the Federal army if they wished to fight. Captain Daniel Ellis, one of the most noted of this class, claims that he piloted ten thousand men to the Federal army in Kentucky and Tennessee. This, however, is probably an exag-

---

[27] O. R., ser. II, vol. I, p. 845.
[28] Ibid., ser. I, vol. LII, pt. II, p. 232. [29] Ibid., ser. II, vol. I, p. 856.

geration. Other famous "pilots" were Spencer Deaton, Seth Lea, and Frank Hodge, of Knox County; Isaac Bolinger, of Campbell; Washington Vann and William B. Reynolds, of Anderson; and James Lane, of Greene. All of these conducted many parties to Kentucky.[30] Captain William B. Reynolds, and no doubt many others, acted as pilot, spy, recruiting officer, and fighter for the Federals, as the occasion demanded. "He would slip into Knoxville, bringing messages and news [to the Federals and to the unionists there], then, ascertaining all that was important about the Confederate army, would slip out and return to Kentucky, leading back a small number of recruits or refugees."[31]

These guides received much valuable assistance from women who collected information for them and for the Federals.[32] One of the most widely known was Mrs. Jeannette Laurimer Mabry, the wife of Colonel George W. Mabry, of Knox County. Although her husband and his family were loyal Confederates, she refused to ally herself with the cause of the South. "She always had the latest news from the front" and was in communication with practically every guide and envoy from the Federal lines.[33]

Not only were East Tennesseans outside of the army loyal to the Union and in constant communication with the Federals, but many in Confederate service were disloyal to the Confederacy. On March 15, 1862, General E. Kirby Smith reported to General Cooper that the soldiers from East Tennessee could not be relied upon to do picket duty; that some of the officers were suspected of being disloyal; and that he believed some of the East Tennessee regiments were disloyal.[34] Later his suspicions were confirmed by the unionists.[35] Captain Robert W. Boone, a great-grandson of Daniel Boone, entered the secret service of the Union army.

[30] Temple, *op. cit.*, pp. 426-27.
[31] *Ibid.*, p. 427.
[32] Humes, *op. cit.*, pp. 364-66.
[33] Temple, *op. cit.*, pp. 427, 428.
[34] *O. R.*, ser. I, vol. X, pt. I, p. 21.
[35] *Parson Brownlow's Book*, p. 219.

After the siege of Knoxville, because of his efficiency as scout, pilot, and spy, he was made captain, with his headquarters at Knoxville. "He operated with his organization or command in East Tennessee, Western North Carolina, Northern Georgia, and South Carolina." During his terms of service, "he belonged to eight different Confederate regiments, serving a part of the time as a private, and part of the time as a commissioned officer," and in both capacities gained much valuable information for the Federals. "He was known then as Charlie Davis, and hundreds of Union officers, piloted by him to the Union lines, rescued by his command from rebel guards or prisons, have good cause to remember him with grateful feelings."[36] Late in January, 1862, J. G. M. Ramsey reported to President Davis that General Crittenden's army refused to serve any longer under him because the soldiers thought that Crittenden was disloyal to the Confederacy and that he had caused Zollicoffer's disaster.[37]

In the spring of 1862, Brownlow was released from prison and sent to the Federals at Nashville. On the way, he managed to collect considerable information concerning the Confederate army. Upon his arrival, this information was given to General Buell.[38]

After June, 1862, many believed that the Confederacy would receive no more help from East Tennessee.[39] Brownlow said that thousands had resolved not to go into the Confederate army; that many of the soldiers under E. Kirby Smith at Cumberland Gap had been forced into the southern army and were unwilling to fight against the Federals; and that the men living at the Gap and for miles up and down the valley were hostile to the Confederacy.[40] Early in

---

[36] Aughey, *Tupelo*, pp. 510-11.
[37] *O. R.*, ser. I, vol. LII, pt. II, pp. 256-57.
[38] *Parson Brownlow's Book*, pp. 381-90.
[39] Chesnut, *Diary*, p. 188; *Weekly Mississippian*, January, 1862.
[40] *Parson Brownlow's Book*, pp. 218-19.

April, 1863, testifying before the Buell Commission, Brownlow informed the Federals that by the summer of 1862 the people in the thirty-two counties in East Tennessee were "five to one on the side of the Union" and that "so long as they [the people in these counties] had anything, they would have contributed it to the government army."[41] When the Confederates lost control of Cumberland Gap, there was a great rejoicing among the East Tennesseans, both at home and in the army, because the "pilots" and other unionists could easily carry news from one to the other.[42]

There seems to be but little doubt that both the order of the Heroes of America and the Peace Society existed in Tennessee at this time. As has already been noted, the "pilots" were aiding the unionists to escape the conscription officers, encouraging the men to join the Federals, and collecting information for the Federal army. Humes says that, during the winter of 1862, "secretly a system had been perfected by which they [persons passing from the Gulf states through East Tennessee to the North] and other refugees were directed from point to point and supplied with means of conveyance by resident citizens—well known to each other and their special friends—whose names were never exposed as helpers in such a work."[43] It was about this time that information concerning the existence of the Peace Society in the army was forwarded to Richmond by Confederate officers who had discovered soldiers belonging to it.[44] After the Confederate losses in 1863, the opposition to the Confederacy increased. By August, conditions were such that General Pillow reported to Inspector General Cooper that no more conscripts could be obtained from Tennessee.[45]

When Burnside entered Knoxville in September, the

[41] *O. R.*, ser. I, vol. XVI, pt. I, p. 674.
[42] Temple, *op. cit.*, pp. 465, 467.   [43] Humes, *op. cit.*, p. 198.
[44] *O. R.*, ser. I, vol. XXVI, pt. II, pp. 555-56.
[45] *Ibid.*, ser. IV, vol. II, pp. 680, 775.

unionists gave him a hearty welcome; and when Longstreet shut him up in the city, East Tennesseans proved their loyalty to the Union by feeding the northern army. The people along the French Broad and its tributaries, who were universally sympathetic with the Union, had hoarded a large part of their bountiful crops. When it was learned that Burnside was shut up within the city, they hastened "to fill little boats with provisions, and silently float them down the river after night to the town. . . . At Knoxville they were checked by a boom devised for this purpose. . . . General Burnside, seeing the immense importance of these supplies, ordered Colonel James A. Doughty, . . . with two or three companies, to take charge of this important work. . . . As fast as received these provisions and supplies were dispatched under the care of trusty men to Knoxville." "Thus the Union people dwelling on the waters of the French Broad, by their generous contributions of supplies, at a critical moment, saved the army of Burnside from starvation and surrender."[46]

Many soldiers were leaving the Confederate army during the fall of 1863 and going over to the enemy. General Rosecrans reported, in September, that under the authority he had previously received, he had organized and mustered into service for twelve months several companies of loyal Alabamans, and that many more deserters were asking for permission to enlist with him.[47] The deserters reported great dissatisfaction among the Confederate troops from Tennessee, Alabama, and North Georgia.[48] In East Tennessee, opposition to the Confederacy continued to increase until the close of the war.

The damage done to the Confederate cause by the unionists in East Tennessee was considerable. The records show

[46] Temple, *op. cit.*, pp. 498-500, 501, 502; Nicolay and Hay, *Abraham Lincoln*, VIII, 175.
[47] O. R., ser. I, vol. XXX, pt. III, p. 529. [48] *Ibid.*

that thirty-one thousand Tennesseans enlisted in the Union army, and Temple and others say there were about four thousand others who fought against the Confederacy. Had these gone into the Confederate army, they would not only have increased the Confederate forces by this number but also have decreased the Federal forces by the same amount. And further, in addition to the loss of the large number of men who enlisted in the Federal army and fought against the Confederacy, from five to ten thousand Confederate soldiers are said to have been required to hold in check the unionists left at home in East Tennessee. Therefore, it is clear that, had these Tennesseans adhered to the Confederate cause, the numbers in the Confederate army would have been increased considerably. Although the direct positive influence of these Union soldiers furnished by Tennessee cannot be estimated exactly in terms of the winning of battles, it seems certain that it was important. Moreover, one cannot estimate the value of the information and other aid given to the Federals by the unionists. Beyond question, the number of desertions not only from Tennessee but also from other states influenced by Tennessee, and the moral support which East Tennesseans gave to Lincoln and the North by showing that almost in the heart of the Confederacy there was a large compact body of men who defied the Confederacy and espoused the cause of the Union, helped to sustain the morale of the Federals and to weaken the morale of the Confederates.[49]

Southwest Virginia

There was much disloyalty in Southwest Virginia, and the Order of the Heroes of America became very powerful in that section. It will be recalled that in Southwest Virginia not more than one-fourth of the people had favored secession. Besides the many strong unionists who never be-

[49] Temple, *op. cit.*, pp. 163, 203, 204.

came reconciled to the war, there were many ignorant mountaineers who since they were in no way concerned with the questions before the people caused no trouble so long as they were let alone. When the conscription act was passed and the unionists and apathetic mountaineers were called on to leave their homes and families and endure the hardships and privations of the army to fight for the Confederacy for which they had no love, it was only natural that they should feel resentment. The result was that many of them resorted to every possible means to keep out of the army, and if they were finally forced to enroll, they deserted at the first opportunity. It was these, their families, and other opponents of the war that became members of the disloyal peace organization.

As the Order of the Heroes of America in Virginia originated in "remote localities, little known and difficult of access, [it] long escaped observation and detection."[50] By 1864, however, it had spread so much and had become so pernicious and formidable in its operations that both the loyal citizens and the Confederate officials became convinced of its existence and began to make investigations.[51]

Henry J. Leory, who was "employed ... as a commissioner to examine persons under arrest by the [Confederate] military authorities," learned through confessions made by a suspected party under military arrest on other grounds, that "combinations [were] being formed among the disloyal in one or more counties for dangerous ends."[52] Brigadier General John Echols, commander of the Department of Southwest Virginia and East Tennessee,[53] aided by Leory and some expert detectives sent from Richmond by the War Department,[54] began to ferret out the members in order to obtain an insight into the character and aims of the order, as well

---

[50] *O. R.*, ser. IV, vol. III, p. 803.
[51] *Ibid.*, p. 802.
[52] *Ibid.*
[53] *Ibid.*, p. 803.
[54] *Ibid.*, p. 802.

as to determine its extent. As soon as a suspected member was discovered, the detectives who themselves were under apparent arrest went to the suspect, and after winning his confidence not only learned that he was a member but obtained the names of other members, the grip, signs, and passwords by which the members of the order might be approached and communicated with. Soon, considerable information was obtained about the society.[55]

The investigation disclosed the existence of a secret, treasonable society known as the Heroes of America[56] which, as already stated, existed in North Carolina[57] and probably in South Carolina and which has been described. The society was found to be very powerful in the southwestern part of the state and to have extended eastward to the bordering counties of the Valley of Virginia.[58] Although, as before stated, it had originated in remote localities, some said it had its headquarters within the Federal lines and had been organized at the suggestion of the Yankee authorities. The Federal officers were well informed as to the character and purpose of the organization and allowed its members to pass freely through their lines. Moreover, as we have seen, the Federals offered, as inducements to those who would join the society, "exemption from military service; protection to their persons and property during the war; and, at the conclusion thereof, participation in the division of the real estate of loyal citizens." The latter promise was emphasized among the ignorant mountaineers.[59] Furthermore, Lincoln's being said to be a member of the organization gave all the more color to such a promise.

It is not known just when the society was first organized in Virginia. Some of the members who were interviewed in

[55] *Ibid.*, pp. 803, 806-9, 810-12.
[56] *Ibid.*, pp. 806-16.
[57] *Ibid.*, p. 809.
[58] *Ibid.*, p. 803.
[59] *Ibid.*, pp. 814-15.

1864 said that it had been in existence for several months.[60] As before noted, the society in Montgomery County, which had about eight hundred members, had been organized in the fall of 1863 by Horace Dean, a North Carolinian who passed through the country on his way home from Richmond.[61]

It seems quite probable that the society was organized in Virginia during the spring of 1862, about the time the conscription act was passed. By March of that year, it was very common to hear the threat made in Russell County that if things did not go to suit the people "there will be found 'plenty of Union men here' "; and " 'If the Confederates do not do (so and so) I'll be for going back to the Union'."[62] The main thing that these people wished the Confederacy to do was to let them alone. No one in that county seemed to be interested in getting men for the army, and the Confederate commander there said men of property had grain, hay, and bacon, but they were more interested in profiteering than in lending a helping hand to the Confederacy. At this time, in Wise County, there were not only many known to be strong unionists but some of the leading men of the county were in communication with the enemy at Pikeville, and had furnished the Yankees with a list of loyal Confederates classified thus: "Such to be killed, such to be transported, such to be sworn and let go." A loyal Confederate who had married into the family of one of the Union conspirators, decided to remain friendly to his father-in-law and act as a detective to protect his friends who were being plotted against. This man reported that Union meetings were being held; that he had a list of twenty-five prominent men who were plotting with the Federals; and that whole districts in Wise County were disloyal.[63]

---

[60] *Ibid.*, ser. I, vol. LII, pt. II, pp. 283-86.
[61] *Ibid.*
[62] *Ibid.*, vol. X, pt. I, p. 360. [63] *Ibid.*, vol. LII, pt. II, pp. 283-86.

At the same time, early in March, the Confederate commander at Lebanon in Russell County, reported that the people from there to the Cumberland Mountains did not intend to fight and urged that martial law be declared over Southwest Virginia in order that the men of conscription age should be compelled to enter the Confederate army or flee the country before they aroused the disloyal to open rebellion against the Confederacy.[64] His advice was unheeded, and, two weeks later, when the Confederates at Lebanon were attacked by the Federals, it was believed that the enemy was guided through the passes by traitors. Three days after this attack, the unionists gathered and marched through the lower part of Lee County "with drums and fifes and with colors flying."[65]

The conscription act was so completely ignored in Southwest Virginia that General Henry Heth felt some radical step must be taken; accordingly, an order was issued, giving notice to all in the counties of Greenbriar, Monroe, Allegheny, Botetourt, Roanoke, Montgomery, Giles, and Bland between the ages of eighteen and thirty-five and subject to military service under the conscription law, who had deserted or had not reported to a conscription officer, that unless they reported to headquarters within five days they would be shot as deserters wherever found.[66]

But the disaffected did all they could to prevent the men from entering the Confederate army. In July, 1862, Brigadier General Heth reported to Colonel G. W. C. Lee, aide-de-camp to the President, that in the southwestern section of Virginia there was a party of "bad, bold and disappointed men ... trying in every way to break down the C. S. army in the section. ... It is my belief that General Floyd is at the head of this organization." These men told the people that the Confederate Congress never had any intention of

[64] *Ibid.*
[65] *Ibid.*, vol. X, pt. II, p. 360.
[66] *Ibid.*, vol. LI, pt. II, p. 584.

compelling all men between eighteen and thirty-five to enter the army; that the government was only appealing to their patriotism; and that the conscription law affected only those already in the army.[67]

Whether this organization was the Heroes of America, and whether Floyd really did head the organization, are mooted questions. It seems quite probable that he did not, but at the same time the organization was fulfilling at least one of the obligations of the Heroes of America. It was reported later that the trouble increased so much when Floyd returned to that section that it was deemed necessary to report conditions to the War Department.[68]

The desertions increased to such an extent that the governor of Virginia ordered that sheriffs, constables, and jailers of the county be used to help the Confederate conscription officers, and all officers enrolling conscripts were given the power to arrest deserters and absentees. Although courts-martial and military executions were resorted to, the number of deserters continued to increase. Later, many of the county officers were found to be members of the Order of the Heroes of America,[69] a fact which accounts for their ineffective service at this time.

After the Confederate military losses in July, 1863, many deserters flocked into the mountainous districts, where they, the renegade conscripts, and other disloyal people, organized into armed bands of from six to fifteen or twenty, and plundered and robbed the loyal citizens for subsistence. Any person who offered criticisms of them soon found his home in ashes, and he was waylaid and beaten or even murdered. As a result of this and the seeming hopelessness of the southern cause, many of the best people in parts of Bedford, Botetourt, Roanoke, Montgomery, Giles, Floyd, Franklin, Pat-

---

[67] *Ibid.*, vol. LII, pt. II, pp. 327-28.
[68] *Ibid.*, p. 327.
[69] *Ibid.*, ser. IV, vol. II, p. 7.

rick Henry, and parts of Pittsylvania were said to be "completely demoralized."[70]

By 1864, between forty and fifty counties of Virginia were within the Federal lines; and in each of these counties, there were about sixty officers who, because of holding a civil office, were exempt from military service; many loyal citizens demanded that these be made to serve in the army now that they had nothing to do. In order to compel them to enter the service, the governor ordered that all male citizens in foreign parts who did not return at once to Virginia would not only be subject to a personal penalty but "their property should be confiscated, and their families sent into the Federal lines."[71]

By 1864, almost all of the people in Montgomery, Floyd, Giles, Pulaski, Scott, and Washington counties were members of the Order of the Heroes of America.[72] No doubt, most of the officers in these, as well as in some other counties, were members of the society and had been elected by the order.[73] The Confederate detectives learned from various members of the society that three justices of the peace in Pulaski,[74] the sheriff in Washington,[75] and the sheriff and two of the police in Montgomery were members and had been elected by the society.[76] General Echols also found that quite a number of officers of the law and some professional men were members.[77]

Some of the prominent members of the Order of the Heroes of America in Southwest Virginia were Daniel H. Hoge, a lawyer living on the North Fork of the Roanoke River in Montgomery County; William Harmon and Captain Callahan, two of the police in Montgomery; Captain

[70] *Ibid.*, pp. 721-22.
[71] *A. C.* (1864), p. 808.
[72] *O. R.*, ser. IV, vol. III, pp. 804-5, 806, 807, 816.
[73] *Ibid.*, p. 803.
[74] *Ibid.*, p. 808.
[75] *Ibid.*, p. 816.
[76] *Ibid.*, p. 815.
[77] *Ibid.*, p. 813.

John Francis, formerly of French's battery, then sheriff-elect of Montgomery County; Randall Cardin, an initiating officer;[78] John Camper, head of the order in Botetourt County;[79] Tom Childress, justice of the peace in Pulaski;[80] John Hampden, sheriff of Washington; and William Boston of the same county.[81] All of these officers had been elected by the order.

The detectives attempted to get in communication with Francis; but when Francis learned a meeting had been planned between them and him, he immediately mounted his horse and rode away without speaking to the detectives. As a result, the other people began to appear restless and the detectives, feeling they were suspected, left town.[82] Again, they came upon Francis at the "still" of the Childress brothers. After much private conversation with various members of the society, Francis, again, rode away. One of the members who believed the detectives to be loyal members of the order, advised them not to go on to Christiansburg as they had planned, because they were suspected as spies.[83]

In August of 1864 the Committee of Safety for Montgomery County appealed to Leory to obtain relief for the loyal citizens. The Committee said that the counties of Montgomery, Floyd, Giles, and other adjacent counties were infested by armed bands of Confederate and Yankee deserters who were burning and taking the property of loyal Confederate citizens. The disloyal bands had fired upon

[78] *Ibid.*, pp. 806-807.
[79] *Ibid.*, p. 810.   [80] *Ibid.*, p. 808.
[81] *Ibid.*, p. 816. Other members of the society were: John Gardner, John Hamilton, sheriff of Washington County, Wm. Dorton of Washington County, Harrison Bowman, one Williams, a wheelwright of Christiansburg, Virginia, Wm. Burnett, a cabinet maker, David P. Hall, Stephen Childress, and Tom W. Terry of Cooper, Virginia.—*Ibid.*, pp. 806-11, 816.
[82] *Ibid.*, pp. 807-808.
[83] Tom Childress, justice of the peace in Pulaski, and his brother owned a brandy distillery. One of the men told the detectives he would like to make some "for Uncle Jeff." Another asked if he would "put something in it"; and he assured them he would.—*Ibid.*

and captured some of the reserve forces and dispersed others. Leory was also warned that the Virginia and Tennessee Railroad was endangered by them.[84] In the fall of 1864, the members of the Heroes of America in two of the southwestern counties organized a state called the "State of Southwest Virginia" for which they elected a governor, lieutenant-governor, and other officers. In the same counties, they "organized a brigade of deserters, for which was chosen a leader who was denominated 'general'."[85] The Committee believed that practically all of the disloyal men in Southwest Virginia were members of the Order of the Heroes of America.[86]

The members of the society told the detectives that the order had members in the army who were actively engaged in encouraging its principles. The members claimed that a majority of the men in the Twenty-second[87] and Fifty-fourth Virginia regiments were members of the society and that the order was widely extending itself in the army near Petersburg.[88] A Dunkard preacher, one of the members, said that most of the Twenty-second Virginia Regiment had deserted from the army, which he thought was a fine thing.[89] General Wilcox, a Confederate, who was stationed near Petersburg, said in January, 1865, that he did not know how long his brigade would hold together as his men were deserting at the rate of fifty every twenty-four hours.[90] Members of the order were believed to have given information on various occasions which caused the frustration of the Confederate plans and contributed to the success and surprises of the enemy. Among the latter was the one which resulted in the surprise and death of General Morgan.

[84] *Ibid.*
[85] *Ibid.*, pp. 803, 814.
[86] *Ibid.*, p. 805.
[87] *Ibid.*, pp. 807, 811.
[88] *Ibid.*, p. 807.
[89] *Ibid.*, p. 811.
[90] Pryor, *Reminiscences*, p. 320.

It was also believed that many members were in General Hood's army. Members were in communication with General Averell when he was in Christansburg.[91]

The detectives were advised by one of the leading members to go into the army of General Lee and spread the doctrines of the order.[92] Lawyer Daniel H. Hoge thought they could render the best service by remaining and trying to secure the election of men to the legislature who favored the calling of a convention of the states to secure peace. Hoge assured them that the order was known to most of the Federal officers and that members of the society were not molested by the Federals. As evidence of this he said that when the enemy was in Blacksburg, the Federals picketed on the mountain opposite his house, but they allowed him to go and come as he pleased. On another occasion, the Federals decided to take a woman's horse but when Hoge assured them that her husband was a member of the order, the horse was not taken.[93] John Camper, head of the order in Botetourt County, assured the detectives that it was one purpose of the order to give to the Federals all the information concerning the Confederates that could be obtained and to protect the deserters from the army. To convince the detectives of the value of the order, Camper said that when the Federals passed through Fincastle where he lived, in answer to his request for a guard, two Federal pickets were stationed at his gate.[94]

The Order of the Heroes of America was so strong and so efficiently organized in Southwest Virginia that it was almost useless to attempt to apprehend deserters and conscripts, or to punish one if he were caught. Many of the members were above conscription age, and had to be dealt with by civil authorities.[95] But since, in so many counties, the courts and jurors were controlled by the society, it was

---

[91] *O. R.*, ser. IV, vol. III, pp. 803, 807, 813.
[92] *Ibid.*, p. 804.
[93] *Ibid.*, p. 809.
[94] *Ibid.*, p. 810.
[95] *Ibid.*, p. 815.

useless to attempt to convict a member on any charge.[96] The situation became so alarming that General Echols and the Secretary of War urged President Davis to ask for the suspension of the writ of habeas corpus, in order to deal with the order.[97] And as we have already seen, it was to suppress the Order of the Heroes of America in Southwest Virginia, North Carolina, and East Tennessee, and other treasonable societies existing in other parts of the Confederacy, that Davis did ask for the suspension of the writ in February, 1864.[98]

[96] *Ibid.*, pp. 803, 814, 815.
[97] *Ibid.*, p. 804.
[98] *Ibid.*, vol. II, pp. 819-20.

SELECTED BIBLIOGRAPHY

I. Primary Materials

Aughey, John H. *Tupelo.* Lincoln, Nebraska, 1888.
Bishop, A. W. *Loyalty on the Frontier, or Sketches of Union Men of the Southwest.* St. Louis, 1863.
Brownlow, W. G. *Sketches of the Rise, Progress, and Decline of Secession (Parson Brownlow's Book).* Philadelphia, 1862.
Chesnut, Mrs. Mary Boykin. *Diary from Dixie.* New York, 1905.
Cleveland, Henry. *Alexander H. Stephens in Public and Private.* Philadelphia, 1866.
Cumming, Kate. *Journal of Hospital Life in the Confederate Army of Tennessee.* Louisville, 1866.
De Leon, T. C. *Four Years in Rebel Capitals: An Inside View of Life in the Southern Confederacy, from Birth to Death.* Mobile, 1890.
Holden, W. W. *Memoirs of W. W. Holden.* 2 vols. Durham, N. C., 1911.
Johnson, H. V. "Documents from the Autobiography of Herschel V. Johnson, 1856-1867," *American Historical Review,* XXX, (January, 1925), 311-36.
Jones, John B. *A Rebel War Clerk's Diary at the Confederate States Capital.* 2 vols. Philadelphia, 1866.
McPherson, Edward. *Political History of the United States of America During the Great Rebellion.* New York, 1864.
Moore, Frank. *The Rebellion Record: a diary of American events, with documents, narratives, illustrative incidents, poetry, etc.* 11 vols. New York, 1861-1868.
Pryor, Sara Agnes (Mrs. Roger A.). *Reminiscences of Peace and War.* New York, 1904.
Rowland, Dunbar. *Jefferson Davis, Constitutionalist: His Letters, Papers, and Speeches.* 10 vols. Jackson, Mississippi, 1923.
Schurz, Carl. *The Reminiscences of Carl Schurz.* 3 vols. New York, 1907-1908.

Senate Reports, 1st Session, 42nd Congress, 1871.
Sherman, W. T. *Memoirs of General W. T. Sherman.* 2 vols. New York, 1875.
Spencer, Cornelia Phillips. *Last Ninety Days of the War in North Carolina.* New York, 1866.
Tribune Almanac and Political Register. 1861-1865. New York, 1868.
War of the Rebellion, The: a Compilation of the Official Records of the Union and Confederate Armies. 130 vols. Washington, 1880-1901.

Newspapers

Eastern Clarion. 1860-1865. Published at Paulding, Mississippi.
Hinds County Gazette, 1860-1865. Published at Raymond, Mississippi.
Natchez Daily Courier, 1860-1862.
The Mississippian, 1860-1865. Published at Jackson, Mississippi.
Weekly Mississippian, 1860-1865. Published at Jackson, Mississippi.

II. Secondary References

American Annual Cyclopedia, for the years 1861-1865.
Ashe, Samuel A'court. *History of North Carolina.* 2 vols. Greensboro and Raleigh, 1908, 1925.
Avery, I. W. *The History of the State of Georgia from 1850 to 1881.* New York, 1881.
Bondurant, Alexander L. "Did Jones County Secede?" *Publications of the Mississippi Historical Society,* I (1898), 104-6.
Callahan, J. M. *Semi-Centennial History of West Virginia.* Charleston, 1913.
Cappleman, Josie Frazee. "Local Incidents of the War between the States," *Publications of the Mississippi Historical Society,* IV (1901), 79-87.
Davis, Jefferson. *Rise and Fall of the Confederate Government.* 2 vols. New York, 1881.
Davis, Wm. Watson. *The Civil War and Reconstruction in Florida* ("Columbia University Studies in History, Economics and Public Law," Vol. LIII). New York, 1913.
Dodd, W. E. *Jefferson Davis.* Philadelphia, 1907.

SELECTED BIBLIOGRAPHY 169

Dowd, Clement. *Life of Zebulon B. Vance.* Charlotte, 1897.
Eckenrode, H. J. *Jefferson Davis.* New York, 1923.
Evans, Clement A. *Confederate Military History.* Vol. II, Atlanta, 1899.
Fleming, Walter Lynwood. *Civil War and Reconstruction in Alabama.* New York, 1905.
──────. "The Peace Movement in Alabama During the Civil War," *South Atlantic Quarterly,* II (April, 1903), 114-24; II (July, 1903), 246-60.
──────. *The Sequel of Appomattox.* New Haven, 1921.
Garner, James W. *Reconstruction in Mississippi.* New York, 1901.
Garrison, George P. *Texas; A Contest of Civilizations.* New York, 1903.
Hamilton, J. G. deRoulhac. *Reconstruction in North Carolina* ("Columbia University Studies in History, Economics and Public Law," Vol. CVIII). New York, 1914.
──────. "Heroes of America," *Publications of the Southern History Association,* XI (January, 1907), 10-19.
Humes, Thomas W. *The Loyal Mountaineers of Tennessee.* Knoxville, 1888.
Knight, Lucian L. *Georgia's Landmarks, Memorials, and Legends.* 2 vols. Atlanta, 1913-1914.
McCarthy, Charles H. *Lincoln's Plan of Reconstruction.* New York, 1901.
Montgomery, Goode. "Alleged Secession of Jones County," *Publications of the Mississippi Historical Society,* VIII (1904), 13-22.
Moore, Albert B. *History of Alabama and Her People.* Chicago, 1927.
──────. *Conscription and Conflict in the Confederacy.* New York, 1924.
Nicolay, John G., and Hay, John. *Abraham Lincoln.* 10 vols. New York, 1917.
Owsley, Frank L. "Defeatism in the Confederacy," *North Carolina Historical Review,* III (July, 1926), 446-56.
──────. "Local Defense and the Overthrow of the Confederacy," *Mississippi Valley Historical Review,* XI (March, 1925), 490-525.

———. *State Rights in the Confederacy.* Chicago, 1925.
Phillips, Ulrich B. *The Life of Robert Toombs.* New York, 1913.
Ramsdell, Charles W. "The Frontier and Secession," *Studies in Southern History and Politics.* New York, 1914.
———. *Reconstruction in Texas* ("Columbia University Studies in History, Economics and Public Law," XXXVI). New York, 1910.
Rhodes, James Ford. *History of the United States,* Vol. III. New York, 1904.
Ridley, Bromfield L. *Battles and Sketches of the Army of Tennessee.* Mexico, Missouri, 1906.
Schwab, J. C. *The Confederate States of America, 1861-1865.* New York, 1901.
Staples, T. S. *Reconstruction in Arkansas* ("Columbia University Studies in History, Economics, and Public Law," Vol. CIX). New York, 1923.
Stephenson, N. W. *The Day of the Confederacy.* New Haven, 1919.
Temple, Oliver P. *East Tennessee and the Civil War.* Cincinnati, 1899.
Thomas, David Y. *Arkansas in War and Reconstruction, 1861-1874.* Little Rock, 1926.
White, Robert. "West Virginia," in Evans, Clement A., *Confederate Military History,* Vol. II. Atlanta, 1899.
Woods, Thomas H. "A Sketch of the Mississippi Secession Convention of 1861," *Publications of the Mississippi Historical Society,* VI (1902), 91-104.

INDEX

ADAMS, Henderson, unionist activity, 32.
Alexander, Col. Edward P., deserters from regiment of, 51.
Alexander, Lieut. W., unionist activity, 71.
Anderson, Charles, unionist activity, 45.
Anderson, Jeff, desertion mentioned, 76.
Armon, N. B. D., disloyal, 67; unionist activity, 68.
Armstrong, H. W., suspect, 67.
Asboth, Brigadier General A. S., report on disloyalty, 40, 41.
Ashe, Samuel A., cited on desertion, 113, 116; on Holden's activity, 118, 119, 122, 129; on Vance and Holden, 120, 121; on Vance-Holden campaign, 132; on peace movement, 128; quoted on extent of volunteering, 109; cited on unionism, 112, 123.
Ashmore, Major John D., activity against traitors, 140, 141; report on desertion, 137, 139.
Aughey, David H., disloyal activity, 93.
Aughey, Rev. John H., cited on unionism, 89-92, 95; quoted, 96; unionist activity, 46, 90-93, 95.
Averell, Gen. W. W., mentioned, 164.
Avery, I. W., cited on desertion, 76; on unionism in Georgia, 10; quoted on flag incident, 74, 75.

BANCROFT, George, unionist activity, 108.
Beck, John, unionist activity, 92, 93.
Benjamin, Judah P., treatment of traitors, 149; mentioned, 36, 109, 145.
Bishop, A. W., cited on secession of Arkansas, 8, 9; on unionism, 25, 38-40, 42; unionist activity, 39.
Blockade, effect of, 21.
Blount, Robert P., investigation of unionism, 54.
Bocock, N. F., investigation of disloyalty, 33.

Bolinger, Isaac, unionist activity, 151.
Bondurant, Alexander, cited on secession of county, 98.
Bonham, Gov. M. L., mentioned, 142.
Boone, Capt. R. W., as spy, 151, 152.
Boren, Henry, unionist activity, 51.
Borland, Col. Solon, treatment of disloyal, 37; mentioned, 36.
Boynton, Prof. E. C., dismissal, 89.
Bradford, Major, mentioned, 114.
Bragg, Braxton, comment on, 126.
Breckenridge, John C., comment on, 126.
Bridgers, R. R., mentioned, 125.
Brown, Gen. E. B., letter on disloyalty, 41, 42.
Brown, Gov. Jos. E., appeal for corn, 19; appeal against traitors, 145; activity against disloyal, 76; complaint about impressment, 18; on conscription act, 15-17, 75; criticism of Davis, 74, 75; effect of criticism, 77; flag incident, 73; in peace movement, 3, 4.
Brown, W. C., Jr., unionist activity, 28.
Brownlow, W. G., book quoted, 5, 6; unionist activity, 5, 6, 149, 152, 153; cited on unionism in Tenn., 143, 146, 147, 149, 151, 152.
Bryan, Guy M., letter to Davis, 49, 50.
Buckner, Gen. S. B., comment on, 126; report on disloyalty, 123.
Buell, Gen. D. C., mentioned, 152.
Burgevin, Adjutant General Edmund, report on disloyalty, 24.
Burke, Theophilus, spying on traitors, 28.
Burnside, Gen. A. E., dealings with disloyal, 154.

CALLAHAN, J. M., cited on unionism, 4, 5; unionist activity, 161.
Campbell, Major, sent against traitors, 148.
Camper, John, unionist activity, 162, 164.
Capers, Col. H. D., activity against disloyal, 83-86.
Cappleman, J. F., cited on unionism, 102.
Cardin, Randall, unionist activity, 162.

[171]

Carroll, Brigadier General W. H., report on disloyalty, 33, 150; on disloyalty in North Carolina, 110.
Carter, W. B., unionist activity, 146.
Chamblee, William, unionist activity, 62.
Chesnut, James, mentioned, 136.
Chesnut, Mary B., cited on currency, 19, 22; on unionism, 95, 152.
Childress, Tom, unionist activity, 162.
Christian, S. H., peace candidate, 125.
Churchill, Rev. Orin, confession about peace society, 130.
Clanton, J. H., activity against peace society, 62; against unionists, 63-66; opinion of troops, 65.
Clark, Gov. H. T., appeal against traitors, 145; opposition to unionists, 103; report on disloyalty, 57, 58; on disloyalty in N. C., 109, 110.
Clemens, Gen. Jeremiah, desertion of, 56; unionist activity, 7, 8.
Clingman, Gen. T. L., mentioned, 140.
Cobb, Gen. Howell, activities against traitors, 63.
Cobb, W. R. W., unionist activity, 61.
Coe, May, unionist activity, 93.
Collins, Jasper, unionist activity, 97, 98.
Conscription law, effect of, 13-15, 38, 39, 41, 42, 45-48, 54, 74, 81, 82, 86, 88, 89, 99, 110-12, 136, 150, 151, 159; officers of law in peace society, 62.
Cooper, Inspector General, mentioned, 153.
Crittenden, Gen. G. B., suspect, 152.
Crump, William, unionist activity, 105.
Cumming, Kate, cited on unionism, 99.
Cunningham, Major, report on disloyalty, 66.
Currency, Confederate, 22.
Curry, J. L. M., mentioned, 61.
Curtis, Samuel R., report on disloyalty, 41.

DAVIS, Jefferson, appeal for corn, 19; criticism of, 17, 20, 94, 136; difficulties with Georgia, 77; with Holden, 119, 120; letter to, 89, 90; mentioned, 13, 16, 36, 122, 165; quoted on treason in North Carolina, 128, 129.
Davis, Nicholas, unionist activity, 7, 8.
Davis, W. W., cited on unionism, 87, 88; on unionism in Florida, 80, 81; quoted, 79.
Davis, Col. W. W., report of desertion, 141.
Dean, Horace, unionist activity, 33, 158.
Deaton, Spencer, unionist activity, 151.
DeLeon, T. C., cited on blockade, 21; on conscription, 14, 15; on soldiers' pay, 22; on unionism in Tennessee, 143, 146.
Dobson, W. W., disloyal, 67.
Dodd, W. E., cited on unionism, 77, 78, 127; on unionism in South Carolina, 136; quoted on treason in North Carolina, 129.
Dorbritz, F. W., unionist activity, 47.
Dowd, Clement, cited on desertion, 117; on Holden's attitude, 111, 129.
Dowd, W. C., spying on peace society, 66.

ECHOLS, Brigadier General John, investigation of disloyalty, 32, 33; activity against disloyal, 156, 157, 161, 165.
Eckenrode, H. J., quoted on Alexander Stevens, 75.
Ellis, Daniel, unionist activity, 150.
Evans, C. A., cited on unionism, 5.

FALKNER, Jefferson, peace society, 28; investigation of disloyalty, 67; mentioned, 68.
Ferguson, Jim, unionist activity, 145.
Fishback, William, unionist activity, 29, 41, 43, 44.
Flanagin, Gov. Harris, speech to disloyal, 49.
Fleming, Walter L., cited on conscription, 14; on desertion, 56; on outrages, 55; on peace movement, 26-32; on Peace Society, 61, 62, 64, 134; on secession of Alabama, 7, 8; on unionism, 6, 57-60, 65-68, 70, 71.
Floyd, Gen. mentioned, 159.
Food, effect of Sherman's raid, 22; scarcity, 21.
Foster, Charles H., unionist activity, 108.

INDEX

Francis, Capt. John, unionist activity, 162.
Frazer, John W., report on desertion, 124.
Fuller, Lieut. T. C., mentioned, 125.

GAITHER, B. S., mentioned, 125.
Galloway, A. N., quoted on secession of county, 98.
Galloway, Charles, unionist activity, 39.
Galt, Major, activity against disloyal, 76.
Gambol, K., unionist activity, 62.
Gantt, E. W., unionist activity, 29, 43, 44.
Gardner, Gen. W. M., activity against deserters, 86.
Garner, James W., cited on unionism, 12, 13, 100, 101, 106.
Gibson, D. W., mentioned, 131.
Giers, J. J., unionist activity, 70, 71.
Gilmer, J. A., mentioned, 125.
Gortney, Washington, unionist activity, 92, 93.
Granger, Gen. Gordon, mentioned, 93.
Grant, U. S., in Order of Heroes of America, 33, 134; mentioned, 71.
Grierson, Col. B. H., report on unionism, 101.
Gross, Sergeant S. W., report on disloyalty in North Carolina, 118.

HALL, Bolling, mention of battalion, 65.
Halleck, Gen. H. W., mentioned, 41.
Hamilton, J. G. DeRoulhac, cited on election, 125; on Holden's activity, 119, 120, 122, 129, 131; on Vance-Holden campaign, 132, 133; on peace sentiment, 129, 130, 134; on unionism, 10, 32, 107, 108, 110, 113, 114, 117.
Hampden, John, unionist activity, 162.
Harmon, William, unionist activity, 161.
Harris, Gov. Isham G., mentioned, 145.
Hawkins, Rush C., on unionism in North Carolina, 107.
Hedrick, Prof. B. S., in Order of Heroes of America, 134.
Heflin, R. S., disloyal, 67.
Heth, General Henry, activity against disloyal, 159.

Hildebrand, A. M., unionist activity, 47.
Hill, A. R., investigation of peace society, 28; activity against disloyal, 68.
Hill, Gen. D. H., mentioned, 117; on disloyalty in N. C., 118, 119.
Hodge, Frank, unionist activity, 151.
Hoge, Daniel H., unionist activity, 161, 164.
Holden, W. W., memoirs cited, 10, 11; mentioned, 127; unionist activity, 10, 11, 111-15, 119, 128-33.
Hollis, Major E., spying on Peace Society, 66.
Honbold, F., unionist activities, 47.
Hood, Gen. John B., mentioned, 164.
Houston, Samuel, criticism of Davis, 49; unionist activity, 11.
House, James, unionist activity, 105.
Hubbard, Col. Richard B., deserters from regiment of, 51.
Humes, T. W., cited on unionism in Tenn., 143, 144, 151; quoted on unionist activity, 5, 6; quoted on unionism in Tenn., 153.
Hunter, Thomas, unionist letter, 123, 124.
Hurlburt, S. A., unionist activity, 76.

IMPRESSMENT, criticism of, 17-19; effect of law, 74, 87, 88, 103, 114, 115.

JEMISON, R. J., unionist activity, 7.
Johnson, Andrew, unionist activity, 70.
Johnson, B. R., report on disloyalty, 96.
Johnson, H. V., cited on conscription, 14; on disloyalty in Georgia, 77; unionist activity, 11.
Johnson, J. L., unionist activity, 134.
Johnston, Gen. A. S., mentioned, 33, 37, 110, 150.
Johnston, Hon. James, mentioned, 66.
Johnston, Jos. E., dealings with disloyalty, 65, 99, 100; mentioned, 16, 79.
Johnston, William, pro-Davis, 112.
Joiner, J. W., unionist activity, 68.
Jones, Col. D. W., investigation of disloyalty, 62.

INDEX

Jones, J. B., cited on conscription, 14; quoted on conscription, 14, 15; on currency, 22; on disloyalty, 127; cited on Alexander Stevens, 77.
Joyner, J. E., description of deserters, 124.

Keith, Capt. J. A., treatment of disloyal, 116.
Kent, William, unionist activity, 28.
Kirk, G. W., encouragement of disloyalty, 134.
Knight, Lucian, cited on secession of Georgia, 9, 10; on unionism in Georgia, 10.
Knight, Methuselah, unionist activity, 96.
Knight, Newton, unionist activity, 97.

Lambert, Thomas, unionist activity, 68.
Lane, Judge George W., unionist activity, 56.
Lane, James, unionist activity, 151.
Lane, Col. J. T., deserters from regiment of, 51.
Lay, Lieut. George, quoted on disloyalty, 120; report on desertion, 125.
Lea, Seth, unionist activity, 151.
Leach, Dr. J. T., peace candidate, 125; unionist activity, 10, 129.
Lee, G. W. C., mentioned, 159.
Lee, Gen. R. E., on desertion in North Carolina, 117, 118.
Leory, Henry J., activity against disloyal, 156, 162, 163.
Lewis, D. P., unionist activity, 7.
Lincoln, Abraham, dealings with disloyal, 146; membership in Order of Heroes of America, 33, 134, 157.
Livingston, Clark, in Peace Society, 62.
Logan, George W., peace candidate, 125.
Longstreet, A. B., mentioned, 154.

Mabry, Col. G. W., mentioned as loyal, 151.
Mabry, Jeannette L., unionist activity, 151.
McCarthy, Chas. H., on unionism, 4, 5.

McClellan, Gen. George B., dealings with disloyal, 146.
McCulloch, Gen. Ben, dealings with disloyal, 51; mentioned, 50.
McGaughey, Major, unionist activity, 70.
McPherson, Edward, cited on unionism, 6.
Magrath, Gov. Andrew G., mentioned, 142.
Magruder, Gen. John B., treatment of disloyal, 49; report on unionism, 52.
Martin, Col., deserters from regiment of, 51.
May, Major, arrest of, 62.
Maynard, Horace, mentioned, 144; unionist activity, 149.
Melton, Major C. D., report on disloyalty, 138, 139; on desertion, 139, 140.
Meroney, E. D., mentioned, 62.
Milton, Gov. John, on disloyalty in Florida, 81-83, 87; on impressment law, 87, 88.
Mitchell, O. M., report of outrages, 55, 56.
Mittanck, Fr., unionist activity, 47.
Montgomery, G., on secession of county, 98; on unionism, 97-99.
Moore, A. B., cited on conscription, 15; on unionism, 8, 80, 81.
Moore, B. F., unionist activity, 133.
Morgan, Gen. John, mentioned, 163.
Musgrove, Lieut. J., in Peace Society, 62.

Negro, plot of insurrection, 38.
Nelson, T. A. R., mentioned, 144.
Nelson, Gen. William, use of spies, 95.

Ooten, James, in peace society, 62.
Owen, R. L., report on unionism, 147.
Owsley, F. L., cited on conscription, 16, 17; quoted on enlistment, 3; on unionism, 4.

Paden, Paul, unionist activity, 96.
Parsons, L. E., disloyal, 67.
Passwords, 27, 29-31, 33, 34.
Paster, J. H., unionist activity, 68.
Patterson, Judge D. T., unionist activity, 149.

Pearson, Judge Richmond, on conscription law, 114, 116; effect of attitude on conscription, 118; attitude toward deserters, 127.
Pemberton, Gen. John C., investigation of disloyalty, 136; mentioned, 100, 137.
Pender, Gen. William D., report on desertion, 117, 118.
Pennington, T. J., unionist activity, 68.
Perryman, D. A., disloyal, 67.
Petrie, E. B., quoted on disloyalty, 135.
Phelan, Sen. James, on conscription law, 89, 90; report of desertion, 103, 104.
Phelps, Commander S. L., unionist activity, 54, 55; mentioned, 96.
Phillips, quoted on impressment, 19; tax-in-kind, 19; on opposition to Confederacy, 20.
Pickens, F. W., mentioned, 136.
Pickens, Paden, unionist activity, 96.
Pickens, Col. Samuel, unionist activity, 149.
Pillow, Gen. Gideon J., report on desertion, 60; on disloyalty, 153; activity against unionists, 99, 100; mentioned, 62.
Poindexter, Judge George, opposition to secession, 13; activity for peace, 100, 101.
Polk, Gen. Leonidas, criticism of, 102.
Poor whites, disloyalty in Florida, 79.
Pope, General John, mentioned, 97.
Powell, J. D., burned in effigy, 98.
Prentice, Wesley, unionist activity, 62.
Preston, Gen., report on desertion, 125.
Price, Linville, quoted on disloyalty, 135.
Pryor, Sara A., cited on blockade, 21; on currency, 22; on desertion, 163; on food scarcity, 22.

QUESTINE, Henry, quoted on disloyal society, 33.

RAMSDELL, C. W., cited on secession in Texas, 11, 12; on unionism, 45.
Ramsey, Dr. J. G., peace candidate, 125.
Ramsey, J. G. M., report on disloyalty, 152.

Rector, Gov. Henry M., address on unionism, 40; mention of treason, 38; treatment of disloyal, 36.
Reece, James, unionist activity, 92.
Reese, George, mentioned, 66.
Revis, Martha, unionist letter, 123.
Reynolds, William B., unionist activity, 151.
Rhodes, J. F., cited on unionism, 5.
Robertson, R. L., disloyal, 67.
Roddy, Gen. P. D., unionist activity, 70.
Rosecrans, Gen. W. S., report on disloyalty, 154; mentioned, 95.
Rowland, Dunbar, cited on Holden, 120; on unionism, 45, 49, 50, 129.
Rungo, C., unionist activity, 47.

SCHOFIELD, Gen. John M., encouragement to disloyalty, 134; mentioned, 41.
Schurz, Carl, memoirs quoted on desertion, 69.
Schwab, J. C., quoted on conscription, 14; cited on currency, 22; on disloyalty, 120; on Holden's activity, 128; on tax-in-kind law, 19, 20; on unionism, 21, 59, 127.
Sebastian, W. K., mentioned, 29, 44.
Secession, opposition to, 4-13.
Seddon, Sec'y Jas. A., complaint about desertion, 103; letter to Vance, 135; mentioned, 32, 33, 83, 116, 118.
Seibels, Col. J. J., peace plan, 66; suspect, 68.
Seward, William H., dealings with disloyal, 146.
Sharkey, Judge W. L., opposition to secession, 13; unionist activity, 100, 101.
Sheets, C. C., unionist activity, 8.
Sherman, W. T., encouragement to disloyalty, 134; activity for peace, 100; in Florida, 80; dealings with unionists, 78; effect of march, 22, 77, 78; mentioned, 16.
Shorter, Gov. John G., on conscription, 57; treatment of disloyal, 63.
Smith, Charles, unionist activity, 105.
Smith, Lieut. E. B., disloyal, 67.
Smith, Gen. E. Kirby, activity against

traitors, 113; report on disloyalty, 50, 151; mentioned, 52, 152.
Smith, W. N. H., mentioned, 125.
Smith, William R., unionist activity, 17.
Smith, William T., disloyal, 67.
Spencer, Cornelia P., cited on peace activity, 128.
Stanton, Edwin M., mentioned, 52.
Staples, T. S., cited on unionism in Arkansas, 43, 44.
Stephens, Alexander H., criticism of Davis, 74, 75; effect of criticism, 77; opposition to the Confederacy, 20, 21; in peace movement, 3, 4; unionist activity, 9, 10.
Stevenson, N. W., cited on conscription, 14, 15; on desertion in N. C., 127; on food raids, 22, 23; on Holden's activity, 129; on opposition to the Confederacy, 21; on unionism, 74, 77, 120, 143.
Streight, Col. A. D., aided by disloyal, 59, 60.
Strickland, William, unionist activity, 83-86.

TAX-IN-KIND law, criticism of, 19, 20; effect of law, 74.
Taylor, Marble Nash, unionist activity, 108.
Taylor, N. G., unionist activity, 147.
Taylor, Gen. Richard, mentioned, 103.
Temple, Oliver P., cited on unionism, 5, 6, 143-49, 151, 153-55.
Terrell, Col. Alexander W., deserters from regiment of, 51.
Thomas, D. Y., cited on Peace Society, 24; on secession of Arkansas, 9; on unionism, 39, 44.
Thompson, Gov. Jacob, opposition to peace movement, 101.
Thompson, John, unionist activity, 95.
Thompson, William, unionist activity, 95.
Toombs, Robert, criticism of Davis, 74, 75; on impressment act, 19.

Turner, Josiah, apposition to war, 112; unionist activity, 10.

VANCE, Zebulon B., opposition to conscription, 16, 17; attitude toward deserters, 127; candidate of disaffected, 112; treatment of disloyal, 116; proclamation against disloyalty, 120, 121; message to Davis, 127; relations with Davis, 122; with Holden, 119, 120, 128-33; in peace movement, 3, 4; mentioned, 141.
Vann, Washington, unionist activity, 151.
Vardenon, Parton, unionist activity, 68.

WALTER, H. W., report of desertion, 104, 105.
Walthall, W. T., quoted on desertion, 61.
Watts, Gov. T. H., on Peace Society, 25, 26; mentioned, 64, 65, 70.
Webb, Gen., investigation of disloyalty, 47-51.
West, A. A., suspect, 67.
West, John L., unionist activity, 79.
White, Robert, cited on unionism, 5.
Wilcox, Gen. C. M., report on desertion, 163.
Wilkerson, Lieut., in Peace Society, 62.
Williams, Mark, unionist activity, 122.
Wood, James, unionist activity, 28, 68.
Wood, Col. W. B., report on unionism, 147-49.
Woods, T. H., cited on unionism, 13, 98, 99.
Worth, Jonathan, activity for peace, 128; quoted on peace, 122, 123; opposition to war, 112; unionist activity, 10, 119.
Wynn, Major, activity against disloyalty, 76.

YANCEY, William, against traitors, 7.
Yerger, Judge J. S., opposition to secession, 13; for peace, 100, 101.

ZULAUF, H., unionist activity, 47.

www.ingramcontent.com/pod-product-compliance
Lightning Source LLC
Chambersburg PA
CBHW030909040526
R18240000001B/R182400PG44116CBX00007B/3